TIL THE WAR IS WON

TIL THE WAR IS WON

How A Reading of Psalm 27 Kept Me Encouraged In Times of Uncertainty

Dr. M. Keith McDaniel Sr.

XULON PRESS

Xulon Press
2301 Lucien Way #415
Maitland, FL 32751
407.339.4217
www.xulonpress.com

Paperback ISBN-13: 978-1-66282-413-5
Ebook ISBN-13: 978-1-66282-414-2

Dedication

~ To every family who lost a love one due to COVID-19 ~

~ To health-care workers who became heroes ~

~ To pastors who preached to empty pews~

~ To teachers and students who studied over digital platforms instead of classrooms~

~ To business owners whose creativity found ways to service your customers~

~To my wife, Latron~

~To my children Keith Jr., Savion, Madison, and Kensley~

Table of Contents

Introduction ix

Chapter One: The Coronavirus and the Crisis It Caused 1

Chapter Two: The Talk 19

Chapter Three: One Thing 49

Chapter Four: I am Not My Pain 65

Chapter Five: Life On Pause 83

Chapter Six: Saying Yes to Life, No Matter What 107

Chapter Seven: Good Courage 121

Chapter Eight: Affirmations According to Psalm 27 145

Introduction

Under normal circumstances you seldom think about breathing. It is something most of us take for granted. That is, until it becomes hard to do. 2020 was one of those kind of years for me. It became hard to breathe. The pandemic, the social unrest, the protests, churches closing, and the world shutting down all at the same time made the year one of the most challenging years of my life. And yet I do not believe that its only impacts were negative. It was a year where I was able to make new dedication regarding my health. It was a year where I was able to think differently as it relates to God and the congregational life of Christians. It was a year that forced me to build resilience as I managed stress. As a believer in God's Word, I understand the importance and the benefit of reflecting upon what the Word of God offers in challenging and uncertain times. My spirit was captured by Psalm 27. It was one of those passages of scripture that I kept going back to during the pandemic and the protests that defined much of 2020.

Psalm 27 is simply titled A Psalm of David. It speaks of trouble, but it also speaks of confidently trusting in the favor of God. It is a psalm of hope and is honest. We are brave at times, and fearful, but always believing. Psalm 27 reminds us that even when we are journeying through dark and difficult days, it is always right to trust God. The world is broken. The world is sinful. We cannot escape the dangers of this world. However, our God is stronger, and He is faithful.

This work is not an exegetical commentary but rather a literary journey of my meditations of life, having lived through a season of pandemic and protest. The themes found in Psalm 27 gave me comfort. Themes like the strength of God, the unceasing presence of God, and the power of belief resonated with me. My hope for you as you read this book is that my reflections will fill your heart with hope and that your spirit will grow stronger in God as you reflect upon your own testimony of how God has kept you during this season of uncertainty. Each chapter of this book comes with an opportunity. As you read my thoughts, I wish to invite you to think through and feel your own. Each chapter concludes with questions, an opportunity to journal, and an action step. I am inviting you to discover what God may have been up to in your life as you have journeyed through this season of instability.

Self-awareness is important. It gives you a better sense of your purpose. It allows you to develop deeper and better relationships with others and with God. This written work affords you the opportunity to create actionable insight that you can use to change your life for the better. As you read, may your introspection and your self-reflection give you the insight to read Psalm 27 in light of your own journey.

Psalm 27 (KJV)

> **1** The LORD is my light and my salvation; whom shall I fear? the LORD is the strength of my life; of whom shall I be afraid?

2 When the wicked, even mine enemies and my foes, came upon me to eat up my flesh, they stumbled and fell.

3 Though an host should encamp against me, my heart shall not fear: though war should rise against me, in this will I be confident.

4 One thing have I desired of the LORD, that will I seek after; that I may dwell in the house of the LORD all the days of my life, to behold the beauty of the LORD, and to enquire in his temple.

5 For in the time of trouble he shall hide me in his pavilion: in the secret of his tabernacle shall he hide me; he shall set me up upon a rock.

6 And now shall mine head be lifted up above mine enemies round about me: therefore will I offer in his tabernacle sacrifices of joy; I will sing, yea, I will sing praises unto the LORD.

7 Hear, O LORD, when I cry with my voice: have mercy also upon me, and answer me.

8 When thou saidst, Seek ye my face; my heart said unto thee, Thy face, LORD, will I seek.

9 Hide not thy face far from me; put not thy servant away in anger: thou hast been my help; leave me not, neither forsake me, O God of my salvation.

10 When my father and my mother forsake me, then the LORD will take me up.

11 Teach me thy way, O LORD, and lead me in a plain path, because of mine enemies.

12 Deliver me not over unto the will of mine enemies: for false witnesses are risen up against me, and such as breathe out cruelty.

13 I had fainted, unless I had believed to see the goodness of the LORD in the land of the living.

14 Wait on the LORD: be of good courage, and he shall strengthen thine heart: wait, I say, on the LORD.

~ CHAPTER ONE ~

The Coronavirus and the Crisis It Caused

As 2019 came to a close, God instructed me to spend all of 2020 preaching and teaching about faith. I had no idea that by the end of February 2020, the world would be facing a pandemic known as the Coronavirus or COVID-19. Nor did I know that by mid-March the United States would come to a screeching halt. However, it became very clear to me why God had given such an instruction as it relates to preaching. There was so much excitement in seeing 2019 come to a close. The joy of a new year was quickly replaced with anxiety. As believers, we are encouraged to walk by faith and not by sight. It seemed that the coronavirus was forcing us to appreciate and evaluate life. It demanded our attention.

It dominated the news cycle. Schools were closed. From elementary to college, students were back at home. Church services were canceled. Grocery stores were empty. Trips were postponed. People were in a panic.

COVID-19 changed people's shopping habits. People were buying groceries and guns in abundance. I had never in my life gone to the store and saw empty meat shelves. I was used to people buying up all of the milk and bread during snow or ice storms. However, the coronavirus had people buying up all the chicken, all the beef, and all the pork; and empty aisles for toilet tissue were a common sight. People were fist fighting in grocery stores over toilet tissue. Gun sales increased during this time. Despite the fact, that I am a senior pastor, I am also a proud owner of a CWP (Concealed Weapon Permit). Don't get me wrong, I believe in prayer and I believe in God, but I also believe that people are crazy, and a pistol will make them calm down faster than my clergy collar. To my surprise, during this time, it was difficult to find ammunition for the pistols I own. These were scary times. No chicken, no steak, no ribs, no pork chops, no toilet tissue, and no ammo. Help me, Jesus.

The impact on the economy was incredible. Cash connects us all. Restaurants were take-out or delivery only. No longer could you go inside the restaurants to sit down and enjoy a meal. Clothing stores turned off their lights and locked their doors. Electronic stores were no longer selling TVs and computers. You couldn't go to a barbershop or a beauty salon. Millions of people were laid off or furloughed. Small business owners worried if they would survive. Many churches had the same worries. Congress negotiated a $1.8 trillion stimulus bill in an effort to keep money in the pockets of small business owners. Unfortunately, it wasn't enough. It was reported that in one week alone, 2.25 million Americans lost their jobs because of this pandemic.[1] Everyone was feeling the stress of being out of work. When people are not working, there is no surplus cash to spend. Everybody felt it, some more than others.

> Even if they didn't lose a job, many workers have had to reduce their

[1] Shane Croucher, American Workers Laid Off Amid Coronavirus Pandemic Face Sleepless Nights 'How Are We Going to Pay Our Bills," https://www.newsweek.com/coronavirus-jobs-unemployment-economy-recession-1493778 Accessed 4/9/2020.

> hours or take a pay cut due to the economic fallout from the pandemic. About a third of all adults (32%) say this has happened to them or someone in their household, with 21% saying this happened to them personally. Most workers who've experienced this (60%) are earning less now than they were before the coronavirus outbreak, while 34% say they are earning the same now as they were before the outbreak and only 6% say they are earning more."[2]

The coronavirus became a worldwide issue. However, in the United States, a disturbing reality began to surface. Unfortunately, COVID-19 had a much more disastrous impact on the African American community than any other. In Chicago, where African Americans comprise a third of the city's population, they accounted for half of the

---

2 Kim Parker, Rachel Minkin and Jesse Bennett Economic Fallout From COVID-19 Continues To Hit Lower-Income Americans the Hardest, https://www.pewresearch.org/social-trends/2020/09/24/economic-fallout-from-covid-19-continues-to-hit-lower-income-americans-the-hardest/ Accessed 2/20/21.

positive cases of COVID-19 and almost three-quarters of the deaths. Likewise, in Milwaukee County, Wisconsin, African Americans make up 70 percent of deaths due to the coronavirus but are only 26 percent of the county's population. According to Sherita Hill Golden, in an article published by John Hopkins Medicine, there were several coronavirus risk factors for people of color. They included living in crowded housing conditions, which made social distancing difficult, inconsistent access to health care, and chronic health conditions, such as diabetes, heart disease, and lung disease.[3] I guess the saying is true: When white people catch a cold, black people get pneumonia.

It seemed that every morning, the breaking news on every channel was the increase in infections and deaths. Older adults and people with severe chronic medical conditions were at higher risk for COVID-19 illness. At the beginning of March, the state of South Carolina, where I live, had no cases of COVID-19. By April 1, there were 1,293 confirmed cases of COVID-19 and twenty-six deaths associated with the

---

3 https://www.hopkinsmedicine.org/health/conditions-and-diseases/coronavirus/covid19-racial-disparities Accessed 6/5/20.

virus.[4] To put the virus in context, by April 2, 2020, there were 216,405 confirmed cases in the United States with 5,136 deaths, and 8,878 people who had recovered. As it relates to the world, 962,977 confirmed cases, 49,180 deaths, and 202,935 people who had recovered.[5] By April 15, South Carolina had over 3,600 confirmed cases and over 100 deaths. By the same date, there were over 600,000 cases in the United States and over 30,000 deaths. Globally, the disease had killed over 131,000 people.[6] The numbers continued to rise. By May 8, 2020, there were over 1 million confirmed cases and over 76,000 deaths related to this virus; these were just the numbers in the United States.[7] By February of 2021, there were over 500,000 people dead due to COVID-19 and over 28 million confirmed cases.[8]

Covid disrupted lives and families. It lingered beyond recovery. Those who recovered still experienced health challenges. Families who supported

---

[4] https://www.livescience.com/south-carolina-coronavirus-updates.html Accessed 4/2/2020.

[5] https://www.bing.com/search?q=how+many+coronavirus+cases&cvid=ee3d7e923cf146f2962b41798b6c3fa6&-FORM=ANAB01&PC=LCTS&adlt=strict Accessed 4/2/2020.

[6] Ibid. 4/15/2020.

[7] Ibid. 5/8/2020.

[8] Ibid. 2/20/21.

covid patients experienced the ongoing psychological trauma of post intensive care syndrome. When a family member is in the ICU it impacts the entire family. Even after that person has recovered, the family may struggle to release the sickness. A wife thinks back to when her husband was in the hospital. A grandchild remembers the sound of alarms and monitors. A daughter, who is grateful that her mother has come home, can't let go of thoughts of her on the ventilator.

Every day they feel the powerlessness of that time. They are thrilled that their love one is finally home. However, they still worry that their love one may get sick again. Maybe their love one has not fully recovered. Every cough frightens them. They know that they don't have to worry about them, but they do anyway. It is called post intensive care syndrome. With all of its tubes and machines the ICU can be a scary environment. Families suffer psychologically even after their love one has recovered. The family may need medical, psychological and emotional help. Caregivers need to be cared for as well. If you are experiencing anxiety, sleepless nights, depression, nightmares and painful flashbacks seek medical attention and if needed a psychologist. Therapy may assist you in accepting the new situation and you may finally be relieved and begin to let go of your loved one's illness.

Social Distancing

Social distancing started to feel like emotional distancing. Isolation breeds anxiety. I began to wonder about what new social norms would emerge. It only takes sixty-six days to form a new habit. I wondered if people would get used to not touching each other, not holding each other, not shaking hands, and embracing one another.

We are by nature social creatures. The Bible says in Genesis 2:18, "It is not good that man should be alone" (KJV). We are also reminded in Ecclesiastes 4:9, "Two are better than one, because they have a good return on their labor" (NIV). Social distancing is such an antithesis of what it means to be human that it almost turned into emotional distancing. We forgot the smiles of loved ones because they wore a mask for an entire year. We used to be huggers; now we walk right past people and don't even shake hands. During the months of March and April of

2020, it was hard to find and buy toilet tissue. A year later, caskets and tombstones were on back order.

Living through a global pandemic had an impact and has left an imprint. People have died alone in the hospitals. School teachers grieved because they knew their students were at home with no food and abusive parents. Healthcare workers put on brave faces and became superheroes. They cried in the dark because they didn't want families and patients to see them exhausted. Pastors found themselves preaching to empty pews. Some senior citizens went an entire year without seeing their grandchildren or even going to church.

My family was impacted by the pandemic. In the early days of 2021 my wife, Latron, tested positive with COVID. She had every symptom: loss of taste, fever, fatigue, and nausea. For fourteen days, she quarantined alone. During that time, she expressed to me thoughts that she was not going to make it. It was difficult being in the same house but not sleeping in the same bed. For two weeks, I slept in the guest bedroom or in my daughter's room. For two weeks, Latron and I ate dinner at the same time but in two different rooms. Social distancing hits differently when you are attempting to quarantine in the same space.

By the grace of God, she was not hospitalized and was able to recover at home. She watched the news coverage of the loss of life, and she wondered if she would be counted in that number. She survived. She is an amazing mother and a thoughtful wife. God's grace kept her, and we are all glad about that. Once cleared and no longer contagious, we both were vaccinated.

There was much discussion about vaccines. I must admit, I was skeptical of taking the vaccine primarily because of the rate of speed in which vaccines against COVID-19 were produced. I wondered what steps were skipped or accelerated in the production? I worried about side effects. Second, I was skeptical because of the historical mistreatment of black bodies via the medical field and quite frankly the US government. The African American community has been disproportionately affected by COVID-19. It is also a community that wants to "wait and see" before getting the COVID-19 vaccine. There continues to be much hesitation about vaccinations.

My vacillation was short lived. I decided to become vaccinated. My wife was also vaccinated.

Why? A few reasons. First, I grew tired of being nervous about being around people, and I no longer want people being nervous about being around me. I wore a mask because I wanted to live. I decided to be vaccinated because I want to live without fear of getting sick or causing someone else to become sick. Second, as a pastor I've buried too many people who died with COVID. I've witnessed the heartbreak of many people I love because of this dreaded disease. Third, we decided to become vaccinated because we love to travel. We want to see the world. Vaccination and international travel are becoming the requirement for many cruise lines and airports. As the world opens up, my family plans on enjoying new things and going to new places and becoming vaccinated gives us the peace of mind that we will not be hospitalized because we decided to emerge from quarantine without protection.

Essential or Non-Essential?

One of the terms that became associated with the pandemic is *non-essential.* In order to encourage social distancing, many businesses shut their doors. Only essential workers were allowed to continue working. Those working in the health-care industry, in banking, as gas station attendants, grocery store workers, restaurant workers, sanitation workers, even owners of liquor stores were allowed to work during the quarantine. They were allowed to remain open because they were deemed as essential service providers. However, there were many people who found themselves at home because they were labeled as non-essential. Wow. Have you ever been labeled as non-essential? It doesn't feel good.

The coronavirus was doing more than putting people out of work. It was causing a crisis in identity. Many were raising the question, "Is my contribution to my community essential or non-essential?" I must admit, my ego was bruised a bit when I learned that churches were not on the list of essential services for communities throughout the country. There was great vacillation regarding churches and the work of the pastor. Were churches to be considered essential or non-essential? Were pastors essential or non-essential? Was communion essential or non-essential? It was amazing to see the number of people criticizing pastors for live streaming services even though they were following social distance practices of ten or less, for inviting members to come by the church to pick up communion or to drive by the church to give their tithes and offerings. The majority of those complaining had never been pastored, nor were they regular church attendees.

I thought to myself, if you are still going to the grocery store to buy groceries, if you are still going by the liquor store to get liquor, if you are still going to the drive through to get a burger, what is the difference in going to the church to pick up communion? What is the difference in a pastor going to the church and streaming a service so that the members at home can be blessed with a weekly instruction from God? If the banker is needed so that you can continue to receive deposits and cash your checks, if the pharmacist is still needed at the window so that you can fill your prescription, and if the news anchor with a film crew can film from their home, using social distancing to make sure you got the news every day, why were pastors being made to feel like non-essential workers?

A Blessing or a Nightmare?

With more families at home and spending more time together, I realized for some this was a blessing, while for others it was a nightmare. Some families used this time to strengthen their bonds. Children were home from school. Family dinners were happening again. I saw families riding bicycles together. I saw family videos on various social media platforms. The stay-at-home order for them proved to be a time to strengthen their family. However, that was not the case for everyone. Domestic violence, child neglect, alcoholism, drug use, as well as sexual and physical abuse increased during this time as well. The stay-at-home order was a mixed bag to say the least.

2020 was the year of cancelations. Weddings were canceled. Flights were canceled. Graduations were canceled. I was in the process of being consecrated as a bishop in the Lord's Church. The initial date set for consecration was canceled. Anxiety and grief were at an all-time high for many. Job security was threatened. People who were in the process of purchasing homes had to cancel their plans, not knowing if they even still had their jobs. Such cancelations brought unexpected grief at the beginning of a new year. This virus forced not only the city, state, or country, but the entire world into isolation.

Pause and Reflect

Take a moment before you move on and think about how the COVID-19 pandemic has affected you personally.

Question 1

What passages of scripture anchored your spirit during the pandemic? How so?

____

____

____

____

____

Question 2

How has it affected the health of your family members? How has it affected your family financially?

____

____

____

____

____

Question 3

How has it affected your local neighborhood?

____

____

____

____

____

Journal: Take a moment a write out your experiences to ensure that what you and your family have lived through is not forgotten.

____

____

____

____

____

____

____

____

____

____

Action:

You have survived a global pandemic. Make a list of blessings you are thankful for in spite of the uncertainty COVID-19 presented. Review your list when you are tempted to doubt in the presence and power of God.

~ Chapter One Notes ~

~ CHAPTER TWO ~

The Talk

The Lord is my light and my salvation; whom shall I fear? The Lord is the strength of my life; of whom shall I be afraid? When the wicked, even mine enemies and my foes, came upon me to eat up my flesh, they stumbled and fell. Though an host should encamp against me, my heart shall not fear: though war should rise against me, in this will I be confident. **—Psalm 27:1–3**

In 1963, James Baldwin wrote a masterpiece called *The Fire Next Time.* There were two essays within the book. The first is "My Dungeon Shook," a letter written to his nephew on the one hundredth anniversary of the emancipation of slaves. Baldwin compared his nephew to the men in his family, men this country had developed an amazing appetite to harass and even kill black men. He encouraged his nephew to channel the anger of that reality into something useful. The second essay within the book is, "Down at the Cross." In this essay, he critiqued the damage Christianity had done to the black community and how he made the pivot away from the church because as he saw it, Christianity seemed to repress his experience as a human being. The book was released during a time of segregation between Whites and Blacks. David said, *"The Lord is my light and my salvation; whom shall I fear"* (Ps. 27:1)?

There is an East African proverb that says I am because we are. It's necessary that we understand that Jesus was an individual, not an isolationist. His ministry was about mobilizing and strategic thinking of how the world order of His day needed to be turn upside down. I thought it a shame that while COVID-19 could keep us from each other, keep us from coming to church, keep us from eating in a restaurant, keep us from visiting our love ones in the hospital, keep us from life as usual; COVID-19 couldn't quarantine hate and racism and bigotry.

What a shame it is that while in the midst of a pandemic, racism could kill you quicker than the coronavirus.

2020 was a year of pandemic and protests that defined and divided the country and, to some degree, the church. During the months of March and April of that year, there was much comparison about 2020 beginning to look like the year 1918. We know that COVID-19 is not the first virus to cause a pandemic in the history of humanity. It will not be the last. In March 1918, a deadly strain of the flu virus was identified in a military camp in Kansas. Six months later, it was worldwide. It would later become known as the Spanish flu. By the time it was over, half the world's population had contracted it. It was perhaps the deadliest pandemic in the history of humankind. During the early months of 2020, there was much comparison of that year with 1918. Photos of people from 1918 resurfaced. They were wearing masks in public, just like we are now. They were told to avoid crowds, just like we are now.

By the time we got to the end of May 2020, it seemed that the year was beginning to look more like 1968, rather than 1918. On April 4, 1968, Dr. Martin King Jr. was assassinated. Two months later in June, Bobby Kennedy was assassinated. Cities like Washington DC, Chicago, Baltimore, Pittsburgh, New York, and other cities experienced riots, deaths, and the destruction of property. Tommie Smith and John Carlos raised their fist in protest at the Olympic games in Mexico City. Three names changed the narrative of the second quarter of 2020. Ahmaud Arbery, Breonna Taylor, and George Floyd reset the algorithm of the news cycles and national attention. In a strange way, 1918 plus 1968 equals 2020. It's bad math, but if you think about it, it makes sense.

The tragic deaths of George Floyd, Ahmaud Arbery, and Breonna Taylor became mainstream news in the middle of a pandemic. Riots, protests, and conversations of systemic racism were now mixing with breaking news updates of COVID-19, the latest job-loss numbers, positive test results, and death totals for the week. I thought to myself, are Christian leaders, particularly pastors, equipped to preach the gospel of Jesus in such a climate—COVID-19 on one end, protests on the other? It is my belief that the church is not God's idea of evacuation but as an instrument of the kingdom of God. It is my fear that if pastors and church leaders do not emerge from this pandemic with a broader view of the kingdom and its earthly assignment, we may become even more irrelevant to the larger context of society.

In February of 2020, in Brunswick, Georgia, Ahmaud Arbery was chased and tracked and gunned down like an animal. In March, Breonna Taylor in Kentucky, an EMT, was murdered by police officers in her home because they raided the wrong house, unannounced without uniform, and then arrested her boyfriend because he attempted to defend his own home, thinking they were intruders. In Minneapolis in May, George Floyd died, to use Killer Mike's expression; "like a zebra caught in the jaw of a lion."[9] The words of James Baldwin ring in my spirit, *Fire Next Time*. All over the country, there were demonstrations and protests. I was born black, and I will die black, but that should not also mean that I must die because I am black. I've been black all my life, not a long time, but long enough to know that racism is real, and racism has always been in the world; it's the star in the narrative of the Divided States of America.

---

[9] Rapper Killer Mike makes tearful speech to Atlanta protesters: 'I am tired of seeing black men die' | The Independent | The Independent. Accessed 5/7/2021.

The Protest of 2020 and Why I Was Inspired

I was so inspired by the protests. To see this movement led by young people was amazing. I was inspired by millennials who demanded change. I was inspired to watch little children participate in the movement. Watching children marching and saying with great passion "No justice, no peace" blessed my soul. It is a huge burden for such young shoulders, but they were brave enough to bear it. I was inspired by the many white faces, who came alongside black faces to cry, to remember, to march, to demonstrate, and to have their voices heard. It felt good as a black man to see that it was not just us, calling for justice.

I was asked the question during the summer of 2020, if Christians should participate in the protest and peaceful demonstrations. My answer was simple. *Absolutely*. Should Christians riot? *Absolutely not*. Should Christians damage and destroy property? *Absolutely not*. There is a difference between rioting and protesting. There is a difference between looting and demonstrating. It is wrong to identify rioters as protestors; the two are *not* the same. Protesting is an inalienable right. Rioting is a criminal act. The two are not the same. The media intentionally and continuously identified rioters as protesters, which was incredibly misleading.

People of faith are people who live in protest. To be Christian is to embrace protest. The Bible, both the Old and New Testaments, gives Christians good reasons to embrace protest as an ordinary form of demonstrating one's faith in God. In Exodus, chapter 1, midwives resorted to civil disobedience to Pharaoh when he commanded that Hebrew boys should be killed at birth. When Moses returned to Egypt with a word from God, "Let my people go," and Pharaoh refused, ten plagues were released in protest of their slavery. Exodus, chapters 3–12, records the story. In Daniel, chapter 3, Shadrach, Meshach, and Abednego refused to bow and worship Nebuchadnezzar's golden image; they stood in protest. When Jesus entered into the temple in John, chapter 2, and saw the poor castigated and price gouging of temple goods, He protested and turned over the tables of the money changers and told them they had turned His Father's house into a den of thieves. Jesus's resurrection from the dead is the ultimate protest against cruelty and oppression. "Despite the qualms Christians may have about the nature, timing, form, or urgency of a particular protest, there is ample biblical evidence to encourage Christians to protest."[10] It was Benjamin D. Wayman who said, "Christian protest witnesses to the reality that all is not well in the world, and it announces the good news that the kingdom of God is near ... Christians protest because God protests."[11] God protested the Egyptians' enslavement of Israel; the ten plagues and the Red Sea are His demonstrations. God protested the burning of the Hebrew boys in Nebuchadnezzar's fire. Their survival and the fourth one who walked with them in the fire is His demonstration. God protested the death of Jesus, and His resurrection on the third day with all power is His demonstration.

Why Protest Is Necessary

Protest is about power and oppression. The right to protest must always be protected. In a democracy, people must always have the right to express their opinions and their disapprovals. Protest is necessary because people lie. People lie in order to stay

---

[10] Benjamin D. Wayman, Why do Christians protest? https://www.christiancentury.org/article/critical-essay/why-do-christians-protest. Accessed 4/10/21.

[11] Ibid 5/7/2021.

in power. People lie because they benefit from the oppression of others. Protest is necessary because there are moments in time when it becomes essential to alter the agenda. No longer should evangelicals look at statistical data regarding unemployment, health disparities, and incarceration and conclude that people are poor because they choose to be or because they are lazy or prone to violence. We must begin to address the deeply embedded systemic issues within our community, namely that of education, housing, and healthcare. Protest is about power and oppression. The people are standing up to the fortresses of power because they understand where the problems reside.

Protest is necessary because there are policies that must become unworkable. Loopholes and technicalities that allow police officers to murder people without penalty should no longer be workable. Protesting is the inalienable right of the people.

Pastor Isaiah Robertson said it best:

> If an unarmed Black man is shot by a police officer, many evangelicals rush to exonerate the shooter and criminalize the victim. The victim's history

> with the law or physical stature is brought into the discussion, implying that somehow the victim deserved to be gunned down. The officer is given the benefit of the doubt while the victim is cast as imminent threat, or only as a tragic example of what happens when one fails to "comply" with law enforcement. Forces of oppression are incessantly defended, and their oppressive actions are explained away and rationalized.[12]

Protest is about identity. The more you understand the passions and the pain and the displeasure of a particular group, the more likely you are to participate in the protest that benefits the group. By identity, I simply mean a shared awareness. Protesting is about emotion. It is about stories. It is about change. Protest happens when an issue becomes personal. It happens when a particular phenomenon negatively affects the way a person lives, their health, their family, or their community.

---

[12] Robertson Isaiah, *Black Church Empowered*, B.C. Empowered Publishing. 2020. p. 134.

People, generally speaking, get involved in protest when they have made an identity connection with regard to the issues at hand. Most black people understand and agree with the sentiment that black lives matter, even if they do not support the organization called Black Lives Matter, because they identify with being Black. Most gay, lesbian, bisexual and transgender people understand the social movement for equal rights because they identify with the oppression of their community. Protest is bringing people with passion into a narrative and calling to action with regard to social or political oppression with which they identify.

It is important to understand that racism is broader than individuals hating or disliking other individuals. Racism is systematic.

> Racism has been part of the American landscape since the European colonization of North America beginning in the 17th century. Even in the post-emancipation era and late in the 20th century, discriminatory laws, social practices, and criminal behavior directed toward blacks

> barred them from owning property or voting, consigned them to segregated schools and housing, and barred them from well-paying jobs.[13]

It was built into systems, such as housing, criminal justice, healthcare, and economics many years ago. Protesting is not about the individual; it is calling attention to the inequities built into the system.

I was inspired by the summer protest of 2020, and yet I was also challenged. Has the church become so comfortable, with air-conditioned sanctuaries, Sunday morning biscuits and coffee between Sunday School and morning worship, the projectors and screens and light shows, that we have forgotten those in the margins because we would rather entertain those in the pews? It seemed to me that there is duality with the Christian Church: white Evangelicals on one side and the historical black Church on the other. And then of course there were those in the middle who said there is no "black Church" or "white evangelical Church"; there is only *the* Church—the body of Christ. For those in the middle, who make

[13] Kathleen Brady, Spartanburg Racial Equity Index, USC Upstate Metropolitan Studies Institute, 2018. p. 7.

statements like this, I understand what they are saying, and I do hear the optimism of their position. However, I conclude that such a statement comes from historical short-sightedness at best or a lack of spiritual and social sophistication at worst.

Christianity is a religion of resistance, not power. There is a distinct difference between the social, political, and spiritual agendas of the white evangelical Church and those who understand systemic oppression and how it affects black and brown people in this country. I long for the day when the body of Christ is singular in her aim to love God with all her heart, mind, and soul and to love her neighbor as she loves herself, but until that day comes, I see the distinction and make no apologies about it. I love the black church. Its worship environment is nurturing, its ministries have rebuilt self-esteem, the congregational life of the people is affirming, and motivate black persons to survive in a hostile world. The psychological and therefore spiritual needs of people of color may be very different than those of the dominant culture. To be honest, the black Church in America exists because the white Church refused to be *the Church*. As long as there are black people in this country and as long as racism continues to exist, so shall the black Church. This is so because black people will always need to be nurtured and affirmed in holy places that belong to them, simply because they live in a hostile world where their progress seems to be a trigger for white rage.

Facts versus Feelings

As protest and demonstrations continued across the country, sparked by the deaths of Breonna Taylor and George Floyd, parents were being forced to talk to their children about the protests they were seeing on television as well as the events that led to them. One morning, while preparing for school, my eight-year-old daughter, Kensley, asked me a most heart-breaking question. Every morning, we watch the local news followed by the national news. During the summer months of 2020, the national news storyline was consumed with narratives of police brutality. After watching the news coverage of George Floyd's murder and the tragic death of Breonna Taylor, Kensley, my eight-year-old daughter looked at me and said, "Daddy, why do the police only kill us?" Race, along with death and sex, are those difficult subjects parents often are nervous to have with their children. I often wondered at what point would Kensley begin to process the fact that the world was not as safe for her as it was for some of her friends.

As a father of four children, Kensley being the youngest, this was not my first time having this conversation. Her three older siblings were aware of and had experienced the pain of racism both in individual and systemic ways. With each child, it seems that they are younger and younger when I had to have "The Talk" with them. As Edwidge Danticat said in her essay "Message to My Daughters," "We are people who need to have two different talks with our black offspring: one about why we're here and the other about why it's not always a promised land for people who look like us."[14] I wondered at what point would the constant image of black death on the national news begin to make her feel inferior or afraid to live in the body God had blessed her with. 2020 was the year Kensley, eight years old began processing death and dying, not simply because of the virus of COVID, but the virus of hatred.

My heart broke into many pieces as she asked the question. I heard the fear in her voice. Her

---

[14] Jesmyn Ward, *The Fire This Time: A New Generation Speaks about Race* (2016) Jesmyn Ward. p.212.

question hit like a weight because I realize there was only so much I could protect her from as a father. As a father, I believe it my duty to protect my family. I've concluded that the only way to protect my children from racism is to help them understand that it exists and that it is opposite of God's heart, as well as giving them the tools necessary to recognize it and reminding them that they must refuse to allow it to define how they see themselves. I reminded Kensley that morning that she was a part of God's beautiful creation.

We prayed, and off to school she went. When she got home, we watched Beyonce's work, *Black Is King* which is a visual album which reimagines the story of "The Lion King" for a new generation who may be in search for meaning, purpose, and even crowns. The film is about the journey of black families throughout time, paying careful attention to the power and spiritual significance of the ancestors. The film highlights the rich tradition of black excellence. It is full of images of black beauty, accented by images and stories that celebrate black legacy, black power, and black pride. The film was extremely uplifting, and it seemed to bring balance to our day.

Music is extremely powerful, and the power of

music is not limited to the Christian faith. Gospel music is not the only music that can inspire the soul. To use Danny Mullins's words, "Music impacts all of humanity because all of humanity has been imbedded with music." Music is about patterns and the anticipation of harmony and melody. I listen to all kinds of music.

I shared my experiences on social media that evening. I made a social media post about my daughter's question, my feelings about her question, and the balance the film brought to our day. To my surprise, a ministry colleague, who happens to be white, responded with a post that sought to disprove Kensley's question. The colleague posted these statistics on my social media page

Number of people shot to death by the police in the US from 2017 to 2020, by race

- **White:** 457 *(2017)* | 399 *(2018)* | 370 *(2019)* | 172 *(2020*)*
- **Black:** 223 *(2017)* | 209 *(2018)* | 235 *(2019)* | 88 *(2020*)*[15]

[15] Romero Jr. Police Kill More Whites Than Blacks is True and it Isn't, https://medium.com/retention/police-kill-more-whites-than-blacks-is-true-and-it-isnt-55102f5206b3 Accessed 4/1/2021

The colleague was quick to point to the facts that more white people are killed by police than blacks. I was outraged. First, because the statistics were flat numbers that do not take into consideration that black people only represent 13.4 percent of the US population. "According to the U.S. Census Bureau, the recorded US population in 2019 was 328.2 million and they've also stated that white people make up 60.4% while African Americans represent only 13.4% ... Based on this, African Americans are 2.4x more likely to be killed by police than their white brothers and sisters."[16]Therefore, the stats presented actually drive home the point little Kensley was feeling.

The second reason why I was outraged was because I did not need facts, especially facts that meant little when placed in proper context. What I needed was the person who I thought understood the challenges of systemic racism and racial bias to feel my pain as a father. There are times when we enter into conversations concerning injustice, and people want to talk about facts and dismiss the feelings or the experiences of another human being. If we only needed more facts, Jesus would have never

---

[16] Ibid. Accessed 4/1/2021.

come. How many times have you found yourself disconnected with people you love because you were trying to prove a fact rather than trying to understand their feelings? How many times did you miss your spouse's heart because you wanted to talk about facts, while they were talking about feelings? How many times did you miss the heart of your child because you were spewing facts, while they were trying to open your heart? How many good friends turn away from you because facts were more important than feelings?

We must never forget that God became a person in Jesus Christ. The incarnation is a doctrinal position of the Church. Emmanuel means God with us. The Church largely accepts that Jesus was fully God and fully human. To believe otherwise would be a heresy. The Church does not support Gnosticism or Docetism, both of which deny the full humanity of Jesus. Because God became a human being, we must take serious the human experiences of living in the bodies God chose for us to live in. The incarnation of Jesus is not an accidental entrance of God into history. He became a human being on purpose. Human beings have feelings, emotions, thoughts, joys, and fears. I've discovered that oftentimes when people introduce facts while you are talking about feelings, it's usually because your feelings are making them uncomfortable. However, the next time someone shares their feelings with you, do your best not to counter their feelings with your facts.

I choose hope. I choose to joyfully take the responsibility of raising beautiful black children. I refuse to leave them to the propaganda machine of white supremacy and black inferiority. Kensley, just like her brothers and sisters before her, will never be ashamed or discouraged to live in the skin they are in. I remind her often that she is beautiful, that she is loved, that she is protected, that God has a plan for her life, and that her mother and father and her entire family are a part of that plan. Several months later, while I was writing this very book, Kensley came into my office and asked me what I was doing. I told her I was writing a new book.

She said to me, "I want to write a book."

I asked her, "What do you want to write about?"

She said, "Brown Girls."

I asked her, "What will you tell them?"

She said, "I will tell them they are beautiful and that no one can judge them on how they look."

I said to her, "You should write it."

Race And the Stories of Our Bodies

Racism is a virus. It's a sickness. It's a disorder, and it is something God hates. "Race is not a history. Race is a story of our bodies, of our churches, of our faith. Race is a story that shapes the ideas of what our bodies are for. It is a word that has de-created our world and us."[17] It was Brian Bantum who said, "We cannot escape the story that has formed us or the stories that shape the world we live in. We cannot be post-racial because race is not about the differences that we see. It is about how those differences have come to form who we think we can be for one another."[18]

David said, "When the wicked, even mine enemies and my foes, came upon me to eat up my flesh, they stumbled and fell. Though an host should encamp against me, my heart shall not fear: though war should rise against me, in this will I be confident." (Ps. 27:2–3) Simply put, it doesn't make sense to live in fear if God is my light and if God is my salvation. It doesn't make sense to walk with God and

---

[17] Brian Bantum, *The Death of Race: Building a New Christianity in a Racial World*, Fortress Press, 2016. p. 5.

[18] Ibid. p.17.

to walk in fear at the same time. I, like David, have confidence.

I am confident that the spirit of God will renew a spirit of decency. Being a decent human being is not supposed to be hard work. It was Maya Angelou who said, "When you know better, do better."[19] It's not impossible to be a decent person. It is not the responsibility of black people to fix white supremacy or racism. If it were up to us, we would have defeated systematic inequality centuries ago. We did not build this racist system; white people did. We do not control this racist system. White people do. It is white people who have quietly agreed to perpetuate white supremacy throughout the history of this country.

I am, however, confident that more of my white Christian friends will speak up and speak out. I am confident that black Christians will continue to be engaged in social issues, seeing them as theological issues. God cares deeply about how we live in this world. Heaven is our home, but we do not live there. We live here, and Jesus told us that He became a human being that we might have life and have it more abundantly (John 10:10). That abundant life

---

[19] Quote by Maya Angelou: "Do the best you can until you know better. Then ..." (goodreads.com). Accessed 5/7/2021.

is not only about eternal life; it is about the here and now also.

Note to Kensley

Kensley, I love you. You are intelligent. You are beautiful. You are my child, and it is my honor to be your father. God made you, and God placed you in this family. You are loved by your mother, Latron, and your sister, Madison, and your brothers, Keith and Savion. You will forever find yourself surrounded by the love of God and the love of this family. God is love, and as a child of God, you should always strive to share that love with others. There are unlimited opportunities in life that will come your way. How do I know? I know this because you have the favor of God on your life. I know this because you have the blessings of your parents on your life. I know this because I see your personality and your strength and your discernment as gifts God has given you to navigate a complicated world. Never forget the following, Kensley:

- *Nothing Is Wrong with You*: Sometimes people are treated unfairly because of the color of their skin. If you ever feel wronged because of the way God made you, please know there is nothing wrong with you. Something is wrong with them.

- *Recognize and Celebrate Diversity*: The world is diverse. If someone ever tells you they don't see color, you should always respond with this, "I am a black person, and when you see me, I want you to see a black *person*." Always remember this, Kensley, God is not color blind, and neither are you. Make the decision to be color brave and not color blind. Celebrate diversity, There are many different ethnic groups across the globe. All of them were created by God, and all them are loved by God. Celebrate the fact that God made us different.

- *Pay Attention*: Anytime you hear me or your mother speak about race or racism, pay attention. Be like a sponge. The world is a complicated place, but I want you to know that it is getting better. Racism is real, but most of the people you will come in contact with are decent people. Find inspiration in people who look like you and are doing amazing things.

- *Always Educate Yourself*: The story of your ancestors does not begin in slavery. You come from a legacy and a people who built civilizations, developed mathematics, organized religious beliefs, and invented many of the things you enjoy today. Guess what, Kensley? All of humanity came from Africa. The first people on this planet looked just like you. Never solely depend on what you learn in school. Read books, watch videos, and ask your parents questions.

- *The World Is a Big Place*: It is not necessary that you take it as is or leave it the same way you found it. Think forward. Be optimistic. Have bold dreams. Laugh out loud. Be yourself and love yourself. You can overcome the impossible. Be the change you wish to see.

- *Wear Your Crown*: It's already bought and paid for.

Pause and Reflect

Take a moment before you move on and think about the following questions.

Question 1

Describe ways you have benefited or ways you have been disadvantaged as it relates to systemic racism? What are your thoughts?

____

____

____

____

____

Question 2

What conversations did you have with your children during the months of protest and pandemic?

____

____

____

____

____

Question 3

How do you maintain positive and constructive relationships with others who see things differently from you?

____

____

____

____

____

Journal: *How has your faith informed you concerning racial equity? Write about a moment when you were either fearful to speak against systemic racism or found the courage to speak out? How might people of faith move beyond speaking and work against injustice and for more equitable communities?*

Action: *Write out and memorize Psalm 27:1–3. As you quote it each day, begin to think through how this passage of scripture applies to your life.*

~ Chapter Two Notes ~

~ CHAPTER THREE ~

One Thing

> "One thing have I desired of the Lord, that will I seek after; that I may dwell in the house of the Lord all the days of my life, to behold the beauty of the Lord, and to enquire in his temple." — Psalm 27:4

During the earlier days of the quarantine, April and May of 2020, I went back and I started looking at a bible study series that I led in 2019. The subject of the bible study dealt with ministry relevance in the 21st century. I thought it was good stuff until april of 2020, when the building was empty. It was then that I realized the fundamental flaw in my teaching in 2019. Everything I spent six weeks teaching my church in 2019, they couldn't use in 2020, because everything I taught them about relevant ministry needed a building to pull it off. I guess that's what happens when you read customer service books and try to apply them to church culture. It only works if the building is open.

David was extremely passionate about being in the house of the Lord. His desire was an impossible task. Yet that is what he desired. Only those born of the tribe of Levi were given access into the inner sanctuaries of the Tabernacle. David was the son of Jesse, born of the tribe of Judah. What David wanted was impossible and yet it was the passion of his heart. When churches across the country began to close their doors in March of 2020, many believers felt like David. Our desire was an impossible task. Sunday morning for many people of faith is the day we collectively worship God and tend to our wounds in community with other people of faith. Many of us could not do that for over a year.

David's desire gave language to his imagination. Imagination is a powerful thing. Imagination is what motivates us to look for the good things that God desires for our lives. A soul without imagination will never achieve God's purpose. One of the positives of 2020 is that it pushed people into a creative space. People began to think beyond themselves. They began to think beyond their self-imposed limitations. Whether it was a new business or a new hobby, it was so refreshing watching people try new things. David's desire sent him on a journey to know God better. That journey was a journey through his imagination. The same God who created the world and whose interactions are recorded in scripture is the same God who gave you your imagination. It is right to use your imagination, to better understand and personalize God's presence in your life. Imagine your life when God fulfills every promise. Imagine what God has in store for you in the next season of your life. Imagine the beauty of your God.

David's language of "to enquire in his temple" also struck me during the pandemic. Every area of ministry was impacted by the closing of the church building and to be honest I worried. I worried about the budget. Churches need to pass the plate when times are good. Most congregations raise their own money to operate. For most congregations that happens on Sunday morning. Churches are not in the profit business. It takes every dollar that comes in to make ministry work. I wondered if people would forget about their churches during this time. I wondered how many churches would survive a season of quarantine. I am so grateful that the members of Macedonia Missionary Baptist Church continued to give and the church was able to keep moving forward.

I worried about the people. Would staying at home and watching the service online be the new normal? I wondered if the membership would become used to distance learning and if so, I needed to embrace distance leadership. I worried about families who were planning graveside funerals. Going through the quarantine of ten people or less, meant that some had to bury the people they loved with limited support. This was traumatic because they felt like they could not give their loved one a proper goodbye. I worried about couples who were planning to wed and were forced to settle for a simple exchange of vows in my office as opposed to the wedding of their dreams.

Pastors are given the awesome task of providing pastoral care to congregations. This includes visiting the sick, wellness checks for seniors, premarital counseling for couples, preparing Bible studies for midweek services, coordinating Sunday morning worship services, working with mortuary services for funerals, and being present for congregants as they experience life. During the pandemic, it seemed like every other day something painful was happening in the life of the people I am so blessed to serve.

I truly love being the pastor of Macedonia Missionary Baptist Church in Spartanburg, South Carolina. We are a highly active congregation in our community. We are a worshipping people. We love the Lord, and we love our community and we love each other (most of the time). During the pandemic, we were hit with incredible loss. We lost good people along the way. Members of the church were experiencing multiple traumas. Every other day, my phone rang with news of surgery, heart attacks, threats of eviction, and/or COVID diagnoses.

Pastoring is a people-centered profession. Without people in the building and without the ability to visit people in the hospital or in their homes, pastoring took on new dynamics. I was not able to do what I am called to do, the way I was used to doing it. I was feeling the weight of being separated from the people I enjoy serving. I felt like I was taking a long walk by myself, and the only acquaintance on the journey was more bad news. I remember one night, one of the deacons called to inform me of a crisis with another family within our ministry. I remember my response. I cried and simply said, "All right," and I hung up the phone. When I hung up the phone, I looked at my wife and said, "It just keeps coming." I got in the bed and just went to sleep. I realized that people of faith were collectively walking through the valley of the shadow of death. Those two words; shadow and death, are incredibly heavy. Shadows suggest darkness; death even darker.

During the quarantined months of 2020, I witnessed our congregation become ***THE*** church despite the fact they could not come to church. We did not fall backwards. We fell forward. We saw the crisis of quarantine as a teachable moment. Despite the fact we had not worshiped together in months, relationships grew stronger, a sense of community seemed more genuine, and the love of Christ shed abroad in our hearts.

King David's desire was to be drawn close to God. David was not a perfect man, but he was a man in love with God. He wasn't always righteous in his behavior, but he was always a worshiper. He was a man of absolute faith in God. Psalm 27:4 reads, "One thing have I desired of the Lord, that will I seek after."

Can I ask you a question? What is the one thing you desire most from God right now? That question must be seriously and thoughtfully answered. Do you know what your soul desires most from God? In order to answer this question, you must have an awareness of your deepest desires. Becoming aware of your deepest desires is essential to understanding who we are as human beings and who God desires that we become.

At different points in our life, our answer to this question may be different, and we need to know that that is okay. When I was a child, I wanted security at night. I was afraid to sleep in my bed alone. In those days, I did not have a TV in my bedroom, and the darkness made me afraid. In my teenage years, I desired most to fit in with my peers. As a husband and father of four, my desire is to be a good father and husband. I want to live long enough so that my family is secure and see my children become successful adults. Each of these desires say something about the person that I was at each time of my life. My point is this: at different points in life, our answer to the question, "What is the one thing you desire most from God right now" may differ and that's okay.

A life of faith should flow from the inside. Make a good practice of paying attention to your soul. Spiritual maturity emerges from a willingness to stay involved with our soul. It is not narcissistic to pay attention to your own soul. It is a requirement for spiritual maturity. During the pandemic days many of us struggled with God because God required of us a deeper yes. This was problematic because some of us were already struggling at the ***YES*** level we were on before the pandemic. What do you do when your desire to draw closer to God, feels like it has backfired?

What Is Your Desire?

David said one thing. He had a lot of problems, but he only desired one thing. David had enemies, problems, and issues, but he only desired one thing. This is what David said: "One thing have I desired of the Lord, that will I seek after; that I may dwell in the house of the Lord all the days of my life, to behold the beauty of the Lord, and to enquire in his temple. (Ps 27:4)" David's desire deserves our reflection. However, it does not require our mimicking. What is your desire? Can I tell you something? One thing can change your life. One moment can change your life. One prayer can change your life. One encounter with God can change your life.

Maybe you need God to strengthen your faith right now. Maybe you need God to bless your finances right now. Maybe you need God to hold your family together right now. Maybe you need God to heal your body right now. Maybe you need God to restore a relationship or help you over what seems to be impossible. Maybe you need God to hide you from temptation. Maybe you need God to encourage you as you struggle through the valley of doubt and despair. Maybe you, like David, believe your desires are impossible. Here is the good news, the impossible is possible despite what it looks like.

What I Asked God For and Why

During the months of protest and pandemic, I asked God for one thing. Guess what I asked God for? I asked God to give me a lifetime supply of grace. Why did I ask for grace? I asked God for grace because it is a game changer. Grace is the undeserved favor of God, and I desire for God to give it to me all the days of my life—not because I want it but because

I need it. Grace is what will allow me to pursue the good work God has called me to do. Grace is what will allow me to live long enough to see my children prosper. Grace is what I need from God to survive in a world where the odds are stacked against me. It's the most important concept in scripture.

Understanding our need for grace is the first step in healing relationships. Grace is something that all of us need. You can always count on the grace of God. The grace of God is what guides us through uncertainty and the unpredictable. We are always in need of God's grace. So I asked God to give me a lifetime supply of His grace. My desire is that the grace of God will never run out in my lifetime.

I asked for the grace of God because I'm convinced it's the only thing I really need. David said in psalm 23:6, "surely goodness and mercy shall follow me all the days of my life." That's my prayer. I desire most of all that the goodness of God, or the favor of God, would follow me all the days of my life. Did you not know that the favor of God shines brightest in moments that are the darkest? My desire is that God would touch every area of my life with his favor. I asked for a lifetime supply of God's grace because I have an imagination. I believe that God is going to do amazing things for me. I need the grace of God to help me imagine every promise in his word coming to pass in my life. God wants you to call upon your imagination. When we imagine God in new ways on a daily basis, amazing things can happen. When we think about Jesus and all that he has done for us our souls shout with gratitude. It is my prayer that God's grace will forever fuel my imagination.

What Is Your One Thing?

We all want to accomplish something in life. Right? Whether you have *big* goals or desire small victories, your imagination needs fuel and drive to take you there. The reality that i encourage you to believe is this, anyone can accomplish anything they dream of. It just takes confidence, the favor of God and a little imagination. Realize your potential and seize your opportunities. Throw away your pre-conditioned notions of you. You lack nothing. Every thing is possible to those who believe. Choose what you want to fill in the canvas of your life, it's blank, tap into your creativity and paint your life a fresh.

What do you desire most from God? Use your voice. No one has your voice, and if you do not use it, it will never be heard. How are you using your voice? How are you using your mind? How are you using your story? How are you using your imagination? Your troubles and your problems and your burdens should not have the leading role in the story of your life. Use your voice, use your mind, use your story, and use your vision. Place your story, your voice, and your mind in the water of your imagination and immerse yourself in the knowledge that God is good and God only wants good for you, while asking God to give you the desires of your heart. The Bible tells us in Psalm 37:4, "Delight thyself also in the Lord, and he shall give thee the desires of thine heart." David said, "One thing I desire and one thing I will seek after." Belief in that one thing is what kept him from giving in and giving out.

Pause and Reflect

Take a moment before you move on and consider the desires of your heart.

Question 1

What is the single most important thing you need God to do in your life?

____

____

____

____

____

Question 2

Do you believe God enough to seek after it?

____

____

____

____

____

Journal:

Write a personal prayer to God, outlining your heart's desire.

____

____

____

____

____

____

____

____

____

____

Action: *Pray this prayer often. Listen for God to speak into your life concerning this desire.*

~ Chapter Three Notes ~

~ CHAPTER FOUR ~

I Am Not My Pain

For in the time of trouble he shall hide me in his pavilion; in the secret of his tabernacle shall he hide me, he shall set me up upon a rock. And now shall mine head be lifted up above mine enemies round about me: therefore will I offer in his tabernacle sacrifices of joy; I will sing, yea, I will sing praises unto the Lord. **—Psalm 27:5–6**

I have often wondered about the lessons we are to learn in troubling times. Our expectation and the realities of life are often out of alignment. And so there are times when our prayer life really is an attempt to manage our expectations. Living includes loss, and with loss comes grief. Pain is a part of life, and yet we do our best to avoid it whenever possible. Everyone will share in the experiences of joy and pain of good days and difficult days. And yet there are positive qualities for suffering. It has a way of narrowing our vision. It brings into focus the things that really matter. I think God allows suffering at times, to bring our life into alignment with the purpose for which He created us.

Pain is a good teacher. The question is, are we good students? How do we navigate a losing season? How do we reframe loss so that we see new opportunities? "Pain is a microphone. And the more it hurts, the louder you get. Suffering isn't an obstacle to being used by God. It is an opportunity to be used like never before."[20] It is never a good idea to ignore pain. I have had a torn rotator cuff. It hurt just to turn a doorknob. I have had golfer's elbow, and I don't even play golf. Pain is not to be ignored; if it is, more damage might result. Painful experiences have so much to teach us. "If you study the history of humankind, you will find that the greatest minds to have walked the earth were those most sensitive to

[20] Levi Lusko, *Through The Eyes of a Lion, Facing Impossible Pain Finding Incredible Power,* W Publishing Group. p. 108.

pain. Pain urged those individuals to ask questions and seek for answers. Pain pushed them to see life from an entirely different perspective."[21]

How well are you managing your pain? There are some experiences that will forever remain with us. As a result, we must manage what God does not remove. You are not your pain. However, your pain is your responsibility. No one else is responsible for managing your pain. Pain management is important because pain keeps us from doing things that we enjoy. In the natural, pain is managed through medication. If your body builds a tolerance to a particular medication your doctor my switch your prescription or may even introduce physical therapies or exercises. Nevertheless, it is up to you to manage your pain.

Many of us have found ourselves in the strange place of trying to coax our soul back to the surface. The tension of the current culture is the struggle between what your soul needs verses what your ministry requires. The tension is truth-telling verses trying to put the right spin on things. Imagine if your

[21] Sofo Archon, Pain is Your Best Teacher, https://theunbounded-spirit.com/pain-is-your-best-teacher/. Accessed 4/8/2021.

soul had a conversation with God, would you be surprised or ashamed of what your soul might say?

Jesus and Suffering

If anybody understood suffering, surely it was Jesus. Over two thousand years ago, Jesus died, calling on his mother in a public lynching. Living during a global pandemic, I realized that all of us were experiencing trauma, but not all trauma is the same. We live in a broken world where something bad can happen at any moment, and bad things often happen, even to Godly people. Jesus knew what suffering felt like long before He got up on the cross. Calvary was not the first time Jesus experienced the traumatic. Isaiah 53:3 says, "He was despised and rejected of men; a man of sorrows, and acquainted with grief." His entire life was about suffering.

- He was born in poverty (Luke 2:1–20).
- He barely escaped the mass murdering of children His own age at the order of King Herod (Matt. 2:16–18).
- He spent forty days in the wilderness in direct conflict with the devil himself (Matt. 4:1–11).

- He was assaulted and rejected in Nazareth, his hometown; even while teaching, they grabbed Him, drove Him out of the temple, and tried to throw Him off the side of the mountain, but He got away (Luke 4:28).
- The people accused Jesus of being mentally ill, maybe even demon-possessed (John 10:20).
- His friends left Him (Mark 14:50).
- He was arrested under false pretense (Mark 14:56–59).
- He was publicly embarrassed (Luke 23:8–12).
- He died naked and alone, hung between two thieves as if He, too, were a common criminal (Mark 15:27–37).

Like Jesus, you who are reading this book may be well acquainted with the tragic. Do you replay traumatic memories from the past time and time again? Do you keep going back to something that upset you? Do you have nightmares, panic attacks, unexplained anger, or mood swings? It may be because your body remembers and your spirit remembers, even if your mind has forgotten. You are not alone. Like countless individuals in the scriptures, you have survived. As a person of faith, you share the legacy of survivors.

The Legacy of Survivors

- Noah—Survived a storm that destroyed everything he knew to be normal (Gen. 6–9).
- Jonah—Survived his own disobedience and the belly of a fish (Jon.).
- Leah—Survived the shameful trick of her father and her husband's neglect (Gen. 29).
- Jochebed—Survived the trauma of releasing her son Moses into a basket and watched him float down the river only to be hired to nurse her own son (Exod. 2).
- Rahab—Survived the Hebrews conquering of Canaan (Josh. 2).
- Deborah—Survived a patriarchal system and became the only female judge in a lawless country (Judg. 4).
- Daniel—Survived the lion's den (Dan. 6).
- Paul—Survived being stoned, beaten, and shipwrecked (2 Cor. 11:25).
- Jesus—Survived the death of the cross (Luke 24).

You are a part of the legacy.

The Worshiping Wounded

Sometimes you have to talk to God while at the same time looking at a wound that won't go away. Worship is always a good place to tend to wounds. Sometimes, the past is never the past. Traumatic events are not really over when they are over. Our faith tradition teaches us that God holds the memory of suffering across the ages in a suffering body. The cross left Jesus injured. We as Christians, do not worship a distant, unapproachable savior. Jesus, knows what it means to be a human being. He understands firsthand what it means to laugh, to cry, to sing, to travel, and to experience the joys and burdens of life. Jesus had friends and enemies. He had good days and difficult days. Hebrews 4:15 says, "For we have not an high priest which cannot be touched with the feeling of our infirmities; but was in all points tempted like as we are, Yet without sin."

Living through the pandemic of COVID-19, surviving in a country where racial inequities still exist, means loss and tragedy have become commonplace. Some of us have lost the possessions of houses and land and business opportunities. Some of us have lost loved ones unexpected. Some of us have lost our routines. Some of us have buried hopes and dreams, and yet we still believe in the power of God. We still believe that our lives have meaning and value.

The traumatic can happen, even to Godly people. We must learn from our losses. It is fascinating to watch a team finish a game that they know they can't win. There is not enough time on the clock to catch up, they are behind by too many points, and yet they keep playing. How do you keep playing when you know you are going to lose? You can learn a lot from a team and even a person who plays to the end and doesn't quit even when they know they can't win. "Your strength doesn't come from winning. It comes from struggles and hardship. Everything that you go through prepares you for the next level."[22]

Listen to what David said: "For in the time of trouble he shall hide me in his pavilion; in the secret of his tabernacle shall he hide me, he shall set me up upon a rock. And now shall mine head be lifted up above mine enemies round about me: therefore will I offer in his tabernacle sacrifices of joy; I will sing, yea, I will sing praises unto the Lord" (Ps. 27:5–6). Notice, when David was in trouble, he didn't

---

[22] Quoted by Germany Kent Winning and Losing Quotes (58 quotes) goodreads.com. Accessed 3/10/21.

find something to keep him preoccupied; he found a hiding place.

I was in a conversation some time ago, and it was said during that conversation that grief is a gift from God. That it is the emotional search for something we have lost. God gives us grief in order to survive the shock of losing, and He uses grief to get us to a place of acceptance. Grief is the vehicle that takes us there. Life is full of losses. We all are familiar with that nagging feeling that something is missing. Life comes with wins, but it comes with losses. David accepted the fact that trouble was and is a part of life, but he also realized that he had a hiding place in God.

A posture of worship is necessary in times like these. David said God would hide him in his pavilion, in the secret of his tabernacle He would hide him. In other words, the presence of God is such a powerful place that when our hearts are hurting and our spirits are crushed, we can hide in God. This is the stabilizing truth in these unstable times. This is David's confidence, and this is David's confession: "For in the time of trouble he shall hide me." It's like Paul saying, "For we know that all things work together for the good of them, who love the Lord. (Rom. 8:28)" It's like James saying, "Knowing this, that the trying of your faith worketh patience, but let patience have her perfect work, that ye may be perfect and entire, wanting nothing. (James 1:3–4)" God uses our trouble to build our confidence and to build our confession.

If you are going to be hidden in God, it means that you must hide all of you in God. "Hide everything in God—your past, your problems, your talents, your potential, your all in all so that neither your enemy, your critics, your friends or any people will only see God in your life. When you hide in God, enemies cannot see you, critics cannot harm you, and praises cannot fool you. They see God not you."[23] To be hidden in God means that you must choose something bigger than yourself to hide in. You cannot hide behind your children because you're bigger than them. You can't hide in a title—you might have to give it back. You can only hide in something that is bigger than you. In the words of Roy Remy, "Talents are not enough to cover. Riches are not enough to cover. Influence is not enough to cover. All these things are not bigger than me. If I must hide myself, I must hide in God for He is bigger than anything in

---

[23] Roy Remy, What Does It Practically Mean To "Hide in God" Apply Radical Truths: WHAT DOES IT PRACTICALLY MEAN TO "HIDE IN GOD" Accessed 3/10/21

this world. Be sure where you place your confidence. Be sure it is enough to cover and hide you."[24]

We Must Trust God

We are imaginative creatures. How do you imagine God when you pray? Do you imagine your prayers as emails waiting to be opened? Do you imagine your prayers as text messages limited to 160 characters? How do you use your imagination when you pray? The gift of your imagination is always available to you. Trusting God makes us all like little children. Little children have huge imaginations. Empty plates overflow with food, in a child's imagination. Stuffed animals listen and breathe in a child's imagination. Imagination is the key in trusting God. Become childlike before God and use your imagination.

We must trust God to hide us when we hurt. Second, we trust God to lift us when we hurt. Listen to what David said, "He shall set me up upon a rock." In other words after the hiding, God has a way of lifting. He will hide you before the lifting. We must go through some things. Before the lift, we must cry

[24] Ibid. Accessed 3/10/21.

sometimes. Before the lift, we must experience the pain and the pressure of life. But thanks be to God, we have a hiding place, and after the hiding, there will be a lifting. This is David's confession. I thank God that He knows how to hide me, and at the right time, God knows how to lift me. Can I tell you something? Life is not trouble free. David is not being unrealistic. Some of us in our faith are not being realistic. I know faith is a supernatural element, but even the supernatural takes place in the realistic. In this life, you will have trouble. In this life, you will experience loss and setback, but when trouble comes, God knows how to hide us, He knows how to lift us, and He knows how to place our feet upon the rock, a solid and a firm foundation.

We must trust that God can hide us when we hurt and that God can lift us when we hurt. Third, we must trust that God will give us a reason to look up when we hurt. Look at what David said, "And now shall mine head be lifted up above mine enemies round about me" (Ps. 27:6). Do not let the people discourage you. Do not let the opinion and thoughts and words of others discourage you. Do not allow people to bring you down. Helen Keller said, "Never bend your head. Always hold it high. Look the world straight in the eye."[25] Max. L. Forman said, "Always hold your head up, but be careful to keep your nose at a friendly level."[26] There are times when we must trust God not because things are traumatic, but we must trust God because things are hectic. Trusting God is necessary during the challenging and trusting God is necessary during the chaotic. Trust God not only when things are bad, but trust God when you find yourself in the midst of busy.

Three Reasons to Trust God

1. Trusting in God reminds us to never take credit for the things God has done. The sin of pride is ingratitude. Proverbs 3:5–6 says, "Trust in the Lord with all thine heart; and lean not unto thine own understanding. In all thy ways acknowledge him, and he shall direct thy paths."

[25] Quoted by Helen Keller—Never bend your head. Always hold it high .... (brainyquote.com) Accessed 05/07/2021

[26] Quoted by Max. L. Forman Always Hold Your Head Up But Be Careful To Keep Your Nose At A Friendly Level @ FriendsQuotation.Com. Accessed 05/07/2021.

2. Trusting in God demonstrates our belief that God is capable of leading us. God has a plan for your life and if you trust him, that plan will unfold as you walk according to His will for your life. Psalm 37:23 reads, "The steps of a good man are ordered by the Lord; and he delighteth in his way."

3. Trusting in God reminds us that the battle is not ours. God will fight your battles. The Bible says in Isaiah 54:17, "No weapon that is formed against thee shall prosper; and every tongue that shall rise against thee in judgment thou shalt condemn. This is the heritage of the servants of the Lord, and their righteousness is of me. Saith the Lord."

To Those Who Lost a Loved One Along the Way

It is my belief that peace and healing will be yours. God is still in control. Peace and healing belong to you. According to Psalm 147:3, "The Lord heals the broken hearted and binds up their wounds." Psalm 34:18 tells us that "the Lord is near to them of a broken heart and saves those of a contrite spirit." I want you to know that it is okay to cry. The Bible tells us in John 11:35 that Jesus wept. Isaiah 26:3 tells us that God will "keep those in perfect peace whose mind is stayed on thee." Keep the positive memories of your loved one alive. Tell their stories. Talk to them. Write to them. Solomon 8:6 tells us that love is stronger than death. I Peter 5:7 says to "cast all your cares upon Him because he cares for you." I believe God cares for you, and I believe that you believe the same.

Pause and Reflect

Take a moment before you move on and think about the ways God has manifested his presence in your life.

Question 1
In what ways has God hidden you?

____

____

____

____

____

Question 2

In what ways has God lifted you?

____

____

____

____

____

Question 3

In what ways has God given you reason to lift your head?

____

____

____

____

____

Journal: *In what surprising ways has God's presence made the difference in your life?*

____

____

____

____

____

____

____

____

____

____

Action: *Take a moment to journal a note to someone you lost to COVID-19. This may be a relative, a family friend, a church member, or a co-worker. Tell them what they meant to you and how you are navigating life now.*

~ Chapter Four Notes ~

~ CHAPTER FIVE ~

Life On Pause

Hear, O Lord, when I cry with my voice: have mercy also upon me, and answer me. When thou saidst, Seek ye my face; my heart said unto thee, Thy face, Lord, will I seek. Hide not thy face far from me; put not they servant away in anger: thou hast been my help; leave me not, neither forsake me, O God of my salvation. When my father and my mother forsake me, then the Lord will take me up. Teach me thy way, O Lord, and lead me in a plain path because of mine enemies. Deliver me not over unto the will of mine enemies: for false witnesses are risen up against

me, and such as breathe out cruelty.
—Psalm 27:7–12

There is a bit of uncertainty in these words that seems to conflict with the words that precede them. Verses 1–6 are filled with confidence in the Lord's supervision and security. However, verses 7–12 carry a sense of uncertainty. He fears rejection and abandonment. In other words, David found himself in an intense state of living in doubt. Have you ever been there? I surely have. As a human being, I acknowledge there are moments that have seemed impossible and insurmountable that have left me exhausted and discouraged. Doubt is a human response to life. It is inescapable.

Regardless of your anointing, your faith, and your experience with God, there will be moments when doubt rolls in on the wheels of inevitability. You cannot escape it. We must deal with doubt. How we decide to deal with it will form the way our lives unfold. As a noun, doubt is defined as "a feeling of uncertainty or lack of conviction." The verb form is similar, meaning to "feel uncertain about."

Doubts are a normal part of our lives, and we live with them most of the time. "When you find yourself questioning some aspect of your faith or the things you believe, invest time and effort in studying what you are being challenged by. Seek to better understand it."[27] Much of my growth as a Christian has come in response to my fears and my doubts. They drove me to study the Word of God. "Use doubt in your own life to move you closer to God. Do not hide or deny it. Doing so will only cause distress and increase the potential of walking away from your faith."[28]

Doubt and unbelief are not the same thing. Your personal history with God is filled with questions. As a matter of fact, you cannot have faith without also having questions. "Doubt is not the absence of faith; doubt is the questioning of faith. You can only doubt what you already believe."[29] Doubt is when you are unsure what you believe, whereas unbelief is the refusal to believe. Doubt occurs because we do not always understand or agree with what God allows. Whereas, unbelief is the rejection that

---

[27] Ed Jarrett, Can a Christian Doubt God and Still Have Faith, Can a Christian Doubt God and Still Have Faith? (christianity.com). Accessed 4/6/21.

[28] Ibid.

[29] Colin Smith, What's the Difference Between Doubt and Unbelief, https://www.crosswalk.com/faith/bible-study/what-s-the-difference-between-doubt-and-unbelief.html. Accessed 4/8/2021.

God even exists. David is a believer in God. I appreciate his honesty because there are times when even believers have doubt and questions.

David desperately needed God to hear his prayer. There have been moments of desperation in my life. Days when my children were in trouble. Days when sickness had attacked my family. Days when I felt overwhelmed with ministry. I have found myself in moments that were unnormal and I needed a miracle. When was the last time you experienced a "But God" moment? Those are the moments in life when everything seems to be against you. There are countless seasons in all our lives where we find ourselves in the depths of unresolvable crisis. It is in those moments of desperation we cry out to God, pleading that God would hear our prayer.

I appreciate David's ambivalence. I appreciate the fact that he put his doubt on paper. David is not the only one in scripture to have moments of vacillation. When God promised Abram, whose name later changed to Abraham, that he would be the father of many nations, he questioned if it were really possible for him to produce a child in his old age (Gen. 17:17). Gideon needed God to confirm his presence with him more than once (Judg. 6:15). Even Jesus on the cross raised the question, "My God, why have you forsaken me" (Matt. 27:46).

Rejections and Kindness

David cried unto God saying, "When my father and mother forsake me, then the Lord will take me up." David, much like the Prophet Isaiah found comfort in the Lord's promise never to leave us alone. Isaiah 41:10 says, "So do not fear, for I am with you; do not be dismayed, for I am your God. I will strengthen you and help you; I will uphold you with my righteous right hand." I want you to know you are not alone. I know the load is heavy. I know the way is dark. I know the trial seems like it will not end, but at this stage in your life, you owe God a praise. Why? Because God did not leave you alone. A crisis, ladies and gentlemen, is not supposed to make us fall apart. Bad news is not supposed to break you down. A season of trial and trouble is not supposed to rob you of your testimony.

There is nothing more depressing than the feeling of being rejected by those we love. We all need acceptance. It is a psychological and a spiritual need. Satan, the enemy of our life, will stop at nothing to exploit the feeling of rejection. Rejection hurts. Learning to cope with this painful reality is a requirement for joyous living. In order to manage the sting of rejection it may be helpful to share your disappointment with the one who rejected you. How you choose to share your feelings depends on your ongoing relationship with them. You may also need to have a constructive outlet for your anger. When you are rejected by people you love, counteract the negative effects of anger and aggression, by finding positive ways to manage your negative feelings. Believe it or not exercise, writing and even dancing may prove useful.

Rejection is not the only thought that came to mind has I read David's words of being forsaken by his parents. I also thought about how the presence of God gives us confidence to complete the undone work of previous generations. There are burdens our children must navigate because we as parents have not completed the assignments given to us. One generation must deal with the ineffectiveness of the previous. Many of the conversations on inequity we are having today are not new conversations. Imagine the joy of a generation finally free from the woes of the previous. May God grant us the courage and the resources to ensure that our children inherit a world and a life far better than the one we inherited. Let us work to fix all that we can fix, so that our children will no longer have to beg God to correct what was in our power to do. Let us all work together to create a more acceptable and inclusive world for our children.

I was disappointed at the fact that too many of us were unwilling to sacrifice a few creature comforts to ensure more of us lived through this pandemic. We were not good neighbors. Something as simple as wearing a mask, became so political, some people stopped thinking about their neighbor and the needs of others. Some of us did not believe that covid-19 was real. Some of us rejected science. Some of us rejected the least of those among us. As a result, too many people died because too many people refused to simply be a good neighbor. The next time you are given an opportunity to be a good neighbor, I pray that you seize the opportunity to be kind.

It is my hope that the church will become a more caring and thoughtful institution post pandemic. As we emerge from this 21st century exile, may the people of God have softer hearts. For far too long has the church been a dangerous place, cloaked in scriptures, robes, rituals, but dangerous. May every church see themselves as a new church plant as they strive toward reentry. Let us truly take up the work of being innovative, rather than recentering ourselves on old beliefs, forms and customs that have only castigated those who would see Jesus. May the unchanging truth of the gospel, change everything we experience in our congregating environments.

The pandemic may have closed the doors of the church, but I hope that it opened our hearts. May we have the courage and the passion to be better neighbors. May the unchurched, people who are unfamiliar with ecclesial jargon, whose theological vocabulary may be limited, but whose curiosity in Jesus has grown during the pandemic, may they find our churches a spiritual home, where they can grow into a disciple of Jesus, and not a clone of the church member they sit beside. May the church begin to understand that Christians are sexual creatures as well. May those whom the church has rejected in the past, find a spiritual community that will be nurturing to their soul. May women who have been called to preach and to pastor, no longer find it exhausting to fit into their calling. In the discussion of equity, classism and sexism must get the same attention as racism. If not, we too are guilty of forsaking our children and again requiring God to do that which we should have done, but have failed because we put religion in front of relationship. May the church become less pious and more personal. After all Jesus said in John 13:35 "by this shall all men know that ye are my disciples, if ye have love one to another."

You Are Not Alone

We are social creatures, and we need each other. Other people make us feel safe and supported. Thank God for people who brought toilet tissue to the house. Thank God for people who picked up an extra bottle of Lysol for you. Thank God for people who sent you silly text messages on days when you were sad. It is easy to become so overcome with our circumstances that we forget that God has a plan and purpose for our lives. It is easy, when in the midst of our pain and loneliness, to forget that it is God who has been holding us and calling us.

God has promised never to leave us. His consistent presence in our life gave us confidence. "Confidence in God makes things possible, it relieves us of worry and mental torment, it brings physical healing into our lives, it enables us to move in the spiritual gifts, to hear the voice of God and to fulfil our calling. Confidence in God opens the door for all the promises of God to come to past in our lives."[30] You cannot lose confidence in God because you lost confidence in a person. You cannot lose confidence in God because you lost confidence in a place. You cannot lose confidence in God because you lost confidence in a thing. God is faithful, able and willing to bring good out of any situation.

Teach Me Your Ways

Living is not always the easiest thing to do, especially if you intend to live Godly. David said in verse 11, "Teach me thy way, O Lord, and lead me in a plain path because of mine enemies." I am not sure what prompted David to make such a request. Did he no longer remember the ways of the Lord? Was he feeling guilt over his sins? Was he spiritually and emotionally out of step with God? No matter

[30] Michael Fackerell, "Confidence in God," Christian-Faith, christian-faith.com. Accessed 2/28/21.

where we find ourselves in life, we must live what we believe according to the Word of God.

It is without a doubt that our worldview shapes our understanding of life. What we believe about God, what we believe about the world, and what we believe about ourselves often gives definition to our understanding of life. As a Christian, we are constantly trying to hold in tension the reality of life and the sacred text that we have come to know as the Word of God. There are times when this is easier said than done. When tragedy hits the life of a believer, it may cause him to reevaluate his beliefs. When the events of life do not line up with our expectations, it may cause us to alter our thinking as it relates to God, the world, others, and ourselves.

One of the many challenges Christians face in living a life of faith is trying to discover the will of God for our lives. Many of us have struggled with trying to determine what God wants us to do. We have struggled to determine where God is. We have struggled with trying to understand why God has allowed certain things to take place. A part of our challenge is centered on the fact that most believers believe that God acts with purpose. As a result, this leads us to make attempts, however feeble, to discern how our own actions might be attuned to God's own actions. Knowing God's will is critical to a life of prayer, spiritual growth, and fruitfulness.

Life at times can be so complicated that it is hard to determine what we believe or why we should believe it. This is especially so for those of us who live in the twenty-first century world. We often struggle when our experiences do not line up with our expectations. When we expect the events of life to happen a certain way, our expectations reveal our beliefs. When the experience does not match the expectation, it influences the beliefs and at times causes us to reevaluate them. For example, if the expectation is to live a long life, but the experience results in a very short life, the belief of longevity as a guarantee changes. If the expectation is to be treated fairly because you treat others fairly, but the experience results in being mistreated by people to whom you have been kind, the belief in reciprocity as being a life rule for everyone changes. What we believe about God, what we believe about others, what we believe about the world and even ourselves is subject to and shaped by our experiences. Nevertheless, we are always to live what we believe.

A Year Of Clarity

When David cried out in verse 11 saying, "Teach me thy way, O Lord" I could not help but raise the question, "What was God teaching us during a year where we were all tested beyond measure?" A year where we went from one extreme to the next. We were bored one minute and anxious the next. We were overworked one week and unemployed the next week. Where the killers of Breonna Taylor were set free, while the killers of George Floyd were arrested, I wondered what God was teaching us.

The year 2020 was a year of uncertainty but it was also a year of clarity. 2020 should have given us 2020 vision. It was clear to me that God was calling the church to remember that God is a God of justice. The opposite of equity is iniquity. Equity is about fairness. It is about ensuring that everyone has what is needed in life to be successful. Inequities occur when biased and unfair policies and practices contribute to the lack of equality. 2020 was a year of divine judgement. This nation desperately needs to find the right path. I was reminded of Isaiah 10:1 which reads, "Woe unto them that decree unrighteous decrees, and that write grievousness which they have prescribed." How did we as a nation forget that God is a God who loves justice?

Justice is one of the attributes of God. God has a deep desire for things to be right. Psalm 89:14 reads "Justice and judgement are the habitation of thy throne: mercy and truth shall go before thy face." Social issues are theological issues. To say that God is a God of justice is to also suggest that God is a God of judgement. Here is the question, do we strive for God's justice or has our desire only been to build our own kingdom? I don't think our lukewarmness is going to go over well with God. Justice is a theme that runs throughout the Bible. It is a theme that reveals God's loving character and our failure to act justly. Psalm 146:6-8 reads, "He is the Maker of heaven and earth, the sea, and everything in them-he remains faithful forever. He upholds the cause of the oppressed and gives food to the hungry. The Lord sets prisoners free, the Lord gives sight to the blind, the Lord lifts up those who are bowed down, the Lord loves the righteous."

God does not support the building of your own empire. We are told in Matthew 6:33 to seek the Kingdom of God. However, far too many of us are busy building our own kingdom. It is easy to tell when you are living in your own kingdom. If you take disagreements personally, that might be a sign that you are building and living in your own kingdom. If you only pray when you need something from God, that might be a sign that you are building and living in your own kingdom. If the only people you can deal with are people who agree with you, you might be building and living in your own kingdom. If you constantly put your wants before the needs of others, you might be building and living in your own kingdom.

According to the parable of Matthew 22:35-40, God expects for us to be better neighbors. Much of the unrest of 2020 was the result of us not being good neighbors to each other. Right paths lead to right places. Are you not tired of spending some much time on wrong roads that lead to wrong places?, I know I am. I am grateful that the Christian journey does not happen on a lonely road. There are others who are traveling along the path with us. I am grateful for the people who take journey with me. I am grateful for the people in my life who have kept me on the right road. People are beings of purpose. "They are moved by passions and desires. They live in pursuit of a treasure to which they have assigned value."[31] Who are the people in your life that you spend the most time around? Are they helpful? Are they harmful? Do they add value to your life, or do they subtract? Are you grateful or regretful for the people who journey the path of life with you?

The Christian faith is grounded in the love of God and the love of neighbor. There are some Christians who are against Christianity, because they have discovered that some Christian communities are hostile environments. Christian discipleship requires that Christians take an active role in learning and reciprocating the love of God. Discipleship is what nurtures our commitment to Christ. The ultimate goal of Christian discipleship is to learn of Christ and to become Christ-like. As we walk with the master, those who journey with us, should make us better.

God desires that our relationship with Him is more transformative and less transactional. A transformative relationship grows from love and inspiration. A transactional relationship is a relationship where one is only in it for themselves. David desperately desired for God to teach him how to live. David did not want to live in his feelings or his fears.

---

[31] Paul David Tripp, *A Shelter in the Time of Storm, Meditations on God and Trouble*, Paul David Tripp, 2009, p. 72.

He wanted to live the life God designed for him. As a result, he understood the need for God to lead him toward a plain path. How many times has that been your prayer? How many times have you asked God, to make the path plain, to take the guesswork out of a life of faith? Right paths are important to people who love God. We do not want to get it wrong. We want to know what the rules are; even if we don't like rules, we don't want to be wrong.

David asked the Lord to lead him in a plain path. In other words, he wanted God to organize his life. He was aware of enemies both internal and external. I will not be super spiritual and tell you that in every decision you will make, you will find a chapter and verse for it in the Bible. As a consequence, I encourage you to pray for the gift of discernment. Discernment is what gives us the ability to follow God's leading. What paths have you asked God to lead you down?

The Plain Path for 2020 and Beyond

- God is a God of Justice Isaiah 10:1
- God does not support the building of your own empire Matthew 6:33

- God expects us to be better neighbors Matthew 22:35-40
- God desires that our relationship with Him is more transformative and less transactional II Corinthians 5:17

What Did God Teach Me in 2020?

There are three things God taught me in 2020. First, God reminded me of the importance of theological flexibility. There were many moments throughout 2020 where I learned how to step out on faith seeing nothing, but believing that somehow my needs would be met. I learned in the storm of 2020 that flexibility was the rule of the day. One morning while studying in my office, a storm battered the city. I heard a loud crashing sound, and the house shook. A tree snapped and hit the roof of my house. The year before, a storm went through the city, and a tree on the opposite end of my home was bent because of the heavy wind. It did not break. It never broke, but it did bend. What I learned was the stronger trees are the ones that move in the storm; whereas, rigid ones are the ones that snap.

When COVID hit, I had to learn how to move, to be flexible, to try new things. I did not force old things to happen in a new environment. Pandemic pastoring pushed me to the limit, but I learned how to be flexible. The more flexible I became, the stronger my roots became. Post-pandemic, I pray that adaptation will be embraced. We should not come out of this season the same way we went into it. Jesus said it best in Mark 2:18–22: "Let us not put new wine in old wineskins."

The second thing God taught me in 2020 was the importance of balance. 2020 was full of unrest, and God was teaching me about rest. It was a difficult lesson to learn because rest involves trust. 2020 caused me to trust God in a different way. I'm a doer. I'm a forward thinker. The pauses and the stops that the pandemic forced us to acknowledge were painful, but I learned how to rest. When the pandemic hit, I thought it was only going to be two weeks in order to flatten the curve. Two weeks turned into a full year. I did not understand how to physically, mentally, or spiritually rest. We live in a culture of now; something is always happening but not during 2020.I learned that rest is not an occasional reward but a prerequisite for greatness. I'm grateful that God is still in control, and even when I feel out of control, I've learned how to relinquish my own control issues to Him.

The third thing that God taught me in 2020 was that grace is a reciprocal gift. I have benefited from the grace of God. Therefore, I should be gracious to others. I always knew this, but 2020 brought it to the surface. Everybody was on edge. Everybody was stressed out. Everybody was living through something they had never lived through before, and everybody was going through it at the same time. 2020 was not the year to wear your emotions on your sleeve. I learn how to extend grace. I understood that human beings were responding to the pandemic in different ways. I reminded myself often that we are all wired differently. My simple maybe someone else's complexity. Grace was given to me, and I have recommitted myself to give grace to others.

Pause and Reflect

Take a moment before you move on and think about the ways God has manifested his presence in your life.

Question 1

Where does your mind go when it wanders off?

____

____

____

____

____

Question 2

In what ways can you become a better neighbor to others?

____

____

____

____

____

Question 3

There is a difference between doubt and unbelief. Describe a moment in your life when you doubted God. What did you learn about yourself and about your relationship with God during that season?

____

____

____

____

____

Journal:

Take a few moments and write about the path of your life you are currently on. How did you get there? What are you learning?

Action:

Work to memorize this affirmation.

> "I will always look up because God is the lifter of my head."

~ Chapter Five Notes ~

~ CHAPTER SIX ~

SAYING YES TO LIFE, NO MATTER WHAT

> I had fainted, unless I had believed to see the goodness of the Lord in the land of the living. **—Psalm 27:13**

Psalm 27 is powerfully irresistible, both because of the way it begins and because of the way it ends. David starts the Psalm by saying in verse 1, "The Lord is my light and my salvation; whom shall I fear?" and he ends the Psalm in verse 13 by saying, "I had fainted, unless I had believed to see the goodness of the Lord in the land of the living." He moved from faith to fear and back to faith again. Life has a way of doing that if you let it, causing us to vacillate, to waver between opinions. It is possible to move from confidence to cowardice, from trusting to trembling, and sometimes that happens on the same day. We can start the day one way and end the day another way. We can start the year one way and end the year another way. Life is about transitions. It is about movement.

In 1946, Viktor Frankl, a renowned psychiatrist, chronicled his experience as a prisoner in Nazi concentration camps during World War II. He titled his writings, *Man's Search for Meaning.* Within the pages of that work, he outlined his psychotherapeutic method that called for the ability to identify one's purpose in life. That if one was able to immerse themselves into a positive imagination about the future, they could survive the horror of their current circumstance. He wrote, "The prisoner who had lost faith in the future—his future was doomed. With his loss of belief in the future, he also lost his spiritual hold; he let himself decline and became subject to mental and physical decay."[32] Frankl's suggestion is that he and others survived because they were able to focus on the future.

---

[32] Viktor E. Frankl, *Man's Search For Meaning,* Pocket Books, 1959, 1962, 1984, p. 95.

When we experience the traumatic, retrospective work is important because it gives us the opportunity to think about what happened to us. Introspective work is necessary because it gives us the opportunity to think about how the experience impacted who we are as a person. Retrospective and introspective work are necessary for healing, but the futuristic positive can keep us alive.

The human spirit is resilient. When you have a sense of meaning in life, you are able to bounce back from the tragic. It is called "tragic optimism" or the ability to find hope and meaning in some of the worst circumstances of life. It is, "an optimism in the face of tragedy and in view of the human potential which at its best always allows for: (1) turning suffering into a human achievement and accomplishment; (2) deriving from guilt the opportunity to change oneself for the better; and (3) deriving from life's transitoriness and incentive to take responsible action."[33]

When your imagination is fueled by your faith and the grace of God, you will either no longer notice the obstacles that stand in your way or they will be so greatly diminished, that they actually work to strengthen your faith as opposed to crushing your

---

[33] Ibid., 162.

faith. We can not manipulate our lives through our beliefs. We can however, become so grateful to God and so focused on our future, that through our imagination we pursue the promises of God and in pursuit of the promises of God, we do not faint, we continue to believe. This is not to suggest that one can be enthusiastic arbitrarily, against all odds and against all hope. Being optimistic is not about commanding joy from thin air. It's about drive. What drives you to be optimistic is found in purpose. You need a reason to be happy. You need a reason to keep believing. People of faith are not people in pursuit of happiness. We are in pursuit of God, but we become happy, along the way, through realizing the purpose, sometimes hidden in a given situation. That purpose allows us to endure suffering.

Giving God a Yes

Psalm 27 is full of fluctuating moods and spiritual reactions that land in a posture of faith but not without test and trial. Giving God a yes is not always easy. This is especially true when life gets hard. When the unfortunate becomes painfully familiar, when yesterday's grief has not left and today's pain is looking for a place to sit down in a heart already full of sorrow, we need more than happiness and more than positivity. We need to believe that we will actually see the goodness of the Lord in the land of the living. David said in Psalm 27:13, "I had fainted, unless I had believed to see the goodness of the Lord in the land of the living." Somehow our ability to hold on to our faith in the midst of trauma and the tragic allowed us to keep saying yes to life in spite of it all. In those moments we need to be baptized again with a fresh spirit of belief.

It is our resilience that actually becomes the means of our resistance. We cannot give into despair and to hopelessness. We cannot decline into the depth of sorrow. We cannot faint. We must believe. David is reminding us that we must always think more about our Savior than we do our struggles. When David found himself surrounded by his problems, he made the decision to focus on His promise. Problems have solutions. Troubles create testimonies. Pain has a purpose. Our ability to hold on to our faith in the midst of trauma and tragedy allows us to keep saying yes to life in spite of it all.

How do we keep saying yes to life in spite of it all? It's about knowing, it's about believing, and it's about seeing. It's about knowledge, it's about hope, it's about manifestation. You cannot allow your circumstance to define who God is for you. You must know, you must believe, and you must see, independent of your situation. We cannot simply believe that God is good in theory; we must know in application. Your circumstance does not define God; it reveals God. This is why your faith has been tested, and because your faith has been tested, your faith can be trusted because you have moved from theory to personal experience.

David said I would have fainted, unless I believed that I would see the goodness of the Lord in the land of the living. Karl Barth said, " 'I believe' means 'I trust.' No more must I dream of trusting in myself, I no longer require to justify myself, to excuse myself, to attempt to save and preserve myself ... I believe—not in myself—I believe in God the Father."[34] The only thing that kept David from giving up and giving out was his continued belief in God. I know there is always something to worry about. There is always something going on. There is always a good reason to wake up in the middle of the night and you can't

[34] Donald K. McKim, *Breakfast with Barth Daily Devotions*, Donald K. McKim, 2019, p.9.

go back to sleep. There is always something to be concerned about; there is no level of life where worry does not exist.

Imagine The Good

David continued to believe. To believe what? To believe that he would see the goodness of the Lord in the land of the living—to see the goodness of God before he died. Here is what I believe; I believe that God is good, and God only desires good for my life, and the good God desires for me to experience, I will experience in this life. That is the kind of imagination you should work to develop for the next season of your life. Immerse yourself into the water of your imagination. Believe that God desires good for your life. Focus your energy around the reasons God has given you to maintain your belief in the author and finisher of your faith. What do you believe? Where does your imagination in God lead you? Our imagination offers us the freedom to be creative. Through our God given imagination, we craft new possibilities, better ideas and a stronger hope for the future.

How do you keep giving life a yes? Believe that your heart is intelligent. Proverbs 18:15 says, "An intelligent heart acquires knowledge, and the ear of the wise seek knowledge." As a result, nothing is impossible with God's help. Philippians 4:13 says, "I can do all things through Christ who strengthens me." Consequently, believe that wisdom lives in your heart and that with it, comes a peace that passes all understanding.

How do you keep giving life a yes? Do what the apostle said in Romans 12:12: "Rejoice in hope, be patient in tribulation, be constant in prayer." According to Jeremiah 29:11, "For I know the plans I have for you," declares the Lord, "plans to prosper you and not to harm you, plans to give you hope and a future." Consequently, you are secure because there is hope in God. You will find rest in His will for your life. You will win every verdict in the court of God's favor.

How do you keep giving life a yes? Live according to Matthew 7:7, where the Lord says, "Ask, and it shall be given you, seek, and ye shall find; Knock, and it shall be open unto you. As a result, believe that God meets all of your needs. Make the same declaration as David who believed he would see the goodness of the Lord in the land of the living.

Feed your imagination with the word of God. According to psalm 1:1-3, "Blessed is the man that walketh not in the counsel of the ungodly, nor standeth in the way of sinners, nor sitteth in the seat of the scornful. But his delight is in the law of the lord; and in his law doth he meditate day and night. And he shall be like a tree planted by the rivers of water, that bringeth forth his fruit in his season; his leaf also shall not wither; and whatsoever he doeth shall prosper." Put your trust in the name of God. God has not forsaken you. God is blessing your steadfastness and God is prospering your hand. Psalm 10:17 reminds us, "Lord, thou hast heard the desire of the humble: thou wilt prepare their heart, thou wilt cause thine ear to hear." God knows the desires of your heart and God is preparing your heart and giving you discernment to hear his word. Psalm 18:2 says, "the lord is my rock, and my fortress and my deliverer; my God, my strength, in whom i will trust." The lord never fails. He always refreshes. Psalm 126:5 tells us "They that sow in tears shall reap in joy."

Pause and Reflect

Take a moment before you move on and think about the words of David as recorded in Psalm 27:13

Question 1

What are some difficulties in your life right now? Do you believe them to be permanent or temporary? How is your belief evidenced in your life right now?

____

____

____

____

____

Question 2

What are some practical ways you can keep an awareness of God's promises in your life every day?

____

____

____

____

____

Question 3

What discipline is needed in your life in order to hold on to what you believe when life becomes difficult?

____

____

____

____

____

Journal

Write about a time in your life when you almost gave up. What gave you the strength to keep going?

____

____

____

____

____

____

____

____

____

Action

Write a vision for your life and your family. Build a prayer life around the vision you have written for your life that includes scripture. Trust in God's ability to keep you and your desires on his mind. Spend time encouraging others as you are waiting on what you believe for yourself.

~ Chapter Six Notes ~

~ CHAPTER SEVEN ~

Good Courage

> Wait on the Lord; be of good courage,
> and he shall strengthen thine heart:
> wait I say, on the Lord. —Psalm 27:14

I think it is important to remind you of this simple truth; you can't quit now. Don't give up on your dreams. Don't give up on your passion. Don't give up on the vision you have for your life, for your family, for your future. No matter how distant your finish line appears to be, you can't quit in the middle; you have to see it through. All the facts are telling you that quitting is smart, that throwing in the towel is the reasonable choice. Yet there is something deep in your spirit that is telling you not to quit. There are people out there that you don't even know exist, who need you. They need your gift. They need your voice. They need your spirit. They need you.

Some of the strongest people I know are people who know all about misery and pain. They know much about defeat; they are acquainted with heartbreak and loss, but they always found a way to believe that trouble doesn't last forever. It was Congressman John Lewis who taught us about good trouble, and it was King David who taught us about good courage. Courage is the willingness to confront uncertainty. When David, in this fourteenth verse, tells us to wait on the Lord and be of good courage, he is reminding us that there is a timing to the things of God. David knew what it meant to have to wait on God. David was anointed as a child; but he didn't become king until he was a grown man. He understood about waiting. There is a weight associated with waiting. There is a skill set needed if you are going to wait.

If you have ever been in the waiting room at the hospital, then you understand the weight that comes from waiting. We are all familiar with the phrase that what goes up must come down. If you throw a ball in the air, no matter how high it goes, it must come down because there is a gravitational pull that works against it. The earth is spinning in circles, but we don't fly off and into outer space because of gravity. It keeps us on the ground. That's why a plane needs a strong engine to take flight and to stay in the air because it has to work against gravity.

A Few Things about Gravity

Gravity Keeps Us Grounded

It's the reason why running downhill is easier than running uphill. It's what makes the jump rope hit the ground again after it goes over your head. Gravity keeps us grounded. There is great value in being rooted and grounded. In order to live a balanced strong life, you must learn to appreciate the ground. You don't want to be ungrounded; you should desire, as the scripture says, to be planted by the rivers of water (Ps. 1).

Staying close to the ground has its benefits. As in basketball:

> Staying low to the ground in basketball is important for a number of reasons and will benefit you on both offense and defense. Having a low

> center of gravity will allow you to be more balanced, act quicker, increase the accuracy of your dribbling and protect the basketball. Players who continually stand up straight the entire game only make themselves less efficient and slower players."[35]

In this season of your life, it's okay to stay grounded, staying low key and close to the ground. Everybody doesn't need to know what you are doing. You don't need a lot fans or even a lot of support. What you need to focus your energy on is the gravity that keeps you grounded when you jump too high.

Gravity also Keeps Us Humble

Gravity requires that you come back down. "Humility isn't the belief that your perspective is worthless. It's the belief that you are a person whose experiences and perspectives have value, situated among a sea of people whose experiences and perspectives also have value. You are not lowly

---

[35] Scott Pisapia, 3 Reasons Why You Should Stay Low While Ball Handling—Basketball Tips (ussportscamps.com) 3/13/21.

or repulsive. The humble perspective is not about looking down or gazing upward—just eye-level appreciation of those who happen to be sharing this planet with you."[36]

To deny gravity might be painful. If you have ever fallen, you know the truth of that statement. Pride goes before a fall.

Gravity Is Real Even Though You Cannot See It

Our hopes and dreams seem to always wrestle and struggle with the invisible. It seems like there is always something getting in the way, always something pushing you, pulling you, and weighing you down. Have you ever felt like you were working on something, dreaming something, believing something, and it felt like something was working against you? It is almost like you're fighting an invisible enemy; there was a force you could not see. Not all weapons are visible. Not all enemies are visible.

Not all traps are visible. There are things working against you that you cannot see. That's why Paul said in Ephesians 6:12, "For we wrestle not against flesh

---

[36] Corinne Purtill, Humility Is The New Grit, What Is Humility, and How Does One Cultivate It? | Forge (medium.com) Accessed 3/13/21.

and blood, but against principalities, against powers, against the rulers of the darkness of this world, against spiritual wickedness in high places." That's why you ought to always whisper a short prayer of protection because there is always something going on that you cannot see. Therefore, you have to ask God to help with the things you don't know about.

Gravity Pulls Us Together

It was Christian McIvor who said, "Not only is it the force that constantly pulls us toward the earth and keeps us from being flung off the planet into deep space, but it also pulls all bodies toward each other ... Gravity keeps us circling through the seasons of our lives and gives us the music of the spheres."[37] So, not only does gravity pull us down, but gravity pulls us together. Have you noticed that in your life, situations keep pulling you back to the same people, like the moon that can't seem to free itself from the gravitational pull of the earth, like the earth that can't free itself from the gravitational pull of the Sun? May the favor of God set you free

[37] Christian Mclvor,The Gravity of God (collegeparkchurch.com) Accessed 3/13/21.

from people who don't like you but constantly feel the need to be close to you. Gravity. May the favor of God set you free from people who use you but don't want you. Gravity. May the favor of God protect you from getting too close to the wrong people who will manipulate your strength to fit their agenda and then throw you away once depleted. Gravity.

Giant-Sized Problems

David knew what it meant to have to deal with giant-sized problems. Let's not forget he killed a giant himself (1 Sam. 17). He knew what it felt to watch the seeds of jealousy sown in life (1 Sam. 18:7). He knew what it felt like to mourn lost friendships (1 Sam. 20). He knew what it felt like to be exiled in the wilderness far from home (2 Sam. 15–20). But David also knew what it felt like to have his joy restored (2 Sam. 6). David knew how to encourage himself in the Lord his God (1 Sam. 30:6). He knew how to get lost in the presence and power of his God (Ps. 23).

If anybody can encourage your heart into believing that waiting on the Lord will pay off, surely it's David. David says in verse 14 that we are to do two things: Wait on the Lord and be of good courage.

If we do those two things, the Word promises us that God will strengthen our hearts. What does it mean to wait on the Lord? Many of us are waiting on God. We are waiting on God to act. We are waiting on God to move. We are waiting on God to answer prayers. We wait on him because we realize that He is God, and we are not.

Right now, some of us are waiting on God to turn our circumstance around, to make a way for us. We are waiting on God to do great things—to open doors and make a way out of no way. We are still waiting on God to do just what He said, but I believe down in my heart that if God said it, that ought to settle it. What does it mean to wait on the Lord? I know they don't offer dial-up internet anymore because dial-up is too slow. I know they don't sell eight-tracks anymore because you don't have time to listen to the whole record just for your song to come back around; that takes too long. I know that we live in the Google, iPhone, and iPad world, and everything is fast and getting faster, but sometimes you just have to wait and believe that God will do just what He said He would do.

To wait on God, means you have come to terms with the notion that you cannot live without God.

Even if you did claim head of household on your taxes, you are still dependent. We depend on God for every breath we take. We depend on God for every beat of our heart. We depend on God for blinking our eyes. We depend on God to keep blood warm in our veins. There has never been a moment in your life when you have been able to live without God, even when you ignored his call and even when you walked away from your assignment. What you now realize is that you are not independent but dependent. To wait on God means that you realize, you cannot do life on your own. It means that you believe God will give you instructions and correction and guidance, as you run this race. But then David says, that we are to be of good courage—as if there is a thing called bad courage and actually, there is.

Bad courage is when you are brave enough to do the opposite of what God told you to do. It takes courage, bad courage, to disobey God. It takes courage, bad courage to do something you know is not right. I shall never forget as a young child, my brother and I, along with some of the neighborhood children, were playing in the woods and found ourselves at the mouth of a tunnel. Bad courage convinced us that it would be a good idea to walk through the tunnel. Walking turned into crawling. Light turned into dark. Laughing turned into crying. We ended up coming out of a manhole on the other side of the neighborhood in what seemed like a forever journey. All I'm saying is there is a difference between good courage and bad courage.

Good courage is standing up for what is right, even if you have to stand by yourself. N. D. Wilson said "Sometimes standing against evil is more important than defeating it."[38] It is the ability to stand and do the right thing no matter the cost. Good courage is obedience to God. Good courage is when you do what God told you to do, not what you want to do, not what you think is right to do, but good courage is doing what God told you to do—when God told you to do it. David said you have to have good courage, and you must wait on the Lord, and in doing so, God will strengthen your heart. I am believing God that God will strengthen your heart. In other words, when you have waited on God, when you trusted God, when you have refused to get in front of God, and when you have settled the issues

[38] Melanie Greenberg The Six Attributes of Courage | Psychology Today. Accessed 3/14/21.

in your mind that you need God, God has a way of strengthening your heart and encouraging your soul.

Here are a few things to consider as you are waiting on the Lord.

Embrace "Rest" As A Part of Your Strategy of Resilience

> Remember the sabbath day, to keep it holy. **—Exodus 20:8**

To wait includes rest. Resilience doesn't require that I have to plow through everything; being resilient doesn't mean I'm always strong. Resilience means that I pay attention to my body and rest and recover. While training, a professional athlete knows how to rest their body so that they can recover. Maybe the reason why God grounded some of your plans is because God intends for you to rest. May the Spirit of the Lord bless the pauses of your life and the stops of your life.

In the early days of the pandemic, many of us wrestled with boredom. We were stuck in the house, doing yard work, painting rooms, planting flowers, and cleaning baseboards. We spent time on YouTube, trying to figure out how to do yoga or how to change oil on the car. We went from the front porch, sat for a little while, only to get up and go to the back porch and do it all over again. We checked emails, downloaded new games on our cellphones, participated in social media games, and created Tik Tok videos. We found ourselves doing everything we could because we were bored.

It was Walter Brueggemann who said:

> In our own contemporary context of the rat race of anxiety, the celebration of the Sabbath is an act of resistance and alternative. It is resistance because it is a visible insistence that our lives are not defined by the production and consumption of commodity goods ... The alternative on offer is the awareness and practice of the claim that we are situated on the receiving end of the gifts of God.[39]

[39] Walter Brueggemann, *Sabbath as Resistance; Saying No to the Culture of Now*, Westminster: John Know Press, 2017, pp. xiii-xiv.

Maybe what God is teaching in these quarantined days is how to sanctify our time. We would do well to rethink, to reimagine, our understanding of the Sabbath, that the Sabbath is not simply a day on the calendar. Christians should reclaim the idea that rest is of God.

The Sabbath is not simply about worship. Sabbath is about sanctifying your time. Somebody said to me once that if somebody wastes ten minutes of your time, the last eight minutes were your fault. Time is the most valuable thing you have because it is the one thing you can never get back. While you are grounded, fight against the urge to do something. Rest and enjoy doing nothing. Let your mind relax. Allow your spirit a chance to reboot and your anointing an opportunity to recharge. I encourage you, dear child of God, to become more intentional about resting and self-care.

Consider Writing Affirmations

An affirmation is a saying that has meaning. You have to use your own words. Find something encouraging to tell yourself every day. Emile Coue told his patients that no matter how sick they were, they were to stand in front of the mirror, and every day they were to say to themselves, "Every Day in every way I am getting better and better." An affirmation is something you repeat in your mind or with your mouth that keeps your spirit encouraged. Here's the question, while you are grounded, what were you telling yourself? When Paul was locked up in prison, instead of doom and gloom, Paul said, "I can do all things through Christ who strengthens me." That is an affirmation. When Nehemiah was rebuilding the walls around Jerusalem and was met with resistance and discouragement, he wrote, "The joy of the Lord is my strength." When your plans, when your hopes, when your desires, have been grounded and you are waiting on God, be intentional about what you say to yourself. I will say more about this later. For now, here are four easy steps in writing your own affirmation.

1. Spend some time reflecting on your personal goals as a human being. What do you desire to accomplish?
2. Use "I am" statements. The affirmation should be personal and passionate. A personal affirmation is about you and only you.

3. Write your affirmation, using only positive words. Focus on what you want and not what you are trying to eliminate. As you write your affirmation, be sure to remove every negative word. Use only positive words.
4. Write your affirmation in the now. Affirmations are about inner experiences. Be present with your words.

Consider a Healthier Way of Life

When you are grounded, turn to things that give you life, not things that take it from you. That means you must reframe your negative thoughts, to see the positive in the midst of the negative. Work to minimize the wrong part of your thinking. There is another way of seeing your experience so that you can imagine the positive that God can make happen, even in the midst of the horrible. You have to choose joy. You have to choose happiness. You have to choose to be optimistic.

You have to eat the right stuff and drink the right stuff so that you will be strong enough to fight the good fight of faith. I guess what I'm saying is when you are grounded, you still have the responsibility to take care of yourself and begin to remove people out of your space who refuse to do the same. Gone are the days of allowing people to abuse your relationship with God. Physical abuse, spiritual abuse, and emotional abuse can no longer be a part of your life story. You are making better decisions about your health, with healthier eating, healthier conversation, and healthier mental stimulation. You have to take care of you.

Consider Celebrating in All Things

Every day you ought to have something to be grateful about. Every day you ought to have something to thank God for. Somebody told me gratitude will train your brain to look for the positive. Even if you cannot celebrate all things, you can choose to celebrate ***IN*** all things. Celebrate while you wait. You don't wait to celebrate; Glory in God in the meantime. Thank God in the meantime. Smile in the meantime. Rejoice in the meantime. Praise Him in advance.

Tomorrow Will Be a Better Day

In almost every sermon I preach, I almost always end up quoting Psalm 30:5, "For His anger is but for a moment, His favor is for life; Weeping may endure for a night, but joy comes in the morning." I have great news for you. Tomorrow will be a better day. If you focus on the morning, you can make it through the night. There are four things Psalm 30:5 teaches us concerning the personality of God.

His Anger Is but for a Moment

There are things that anger God. Be not deceived; your God gets angry, yet his anger is only for a moment. When God is angry, His anger is not like our anger. When people get mad at you, they stop talking to you. They go days without talking, they block your number, and they unfriend you on social media. But I'm glad God doesn't do me like that. I know there have been times when I have angered God, made God upset, and even disappointed God, but God never stopped talking to me, and I'm glad about that. God gets angry, but God does not stay angry. It's against His nature to hold a grudge.

His Favor Is for Life

This is the real reason why His anger is only for a moment: it's because His favor is for a lifetime. God rejoices in you and delights in you and wants to bless you. When God decides to favor you, it is a decision He never takes back. Think about the power of this Psalm. God's favor over your life is for your whole life.

Weeping May Endure for a Night

Crying is a part of life. Pain is a part of life. Weeping may endure for the night, but it is not staying. Sadness is not a resident; it is a visitor. Trouble does not last always. Every storm will eventually run out of rain.

But Joy Comes in the Morning

Can I tell you something? Joy is coming in the morning. Joy is what happens when we allow ourselves to recognize how good things really are. Joy is a fruit of the spirit. Be like the birds that live around my house. Those birds sing when the sun is shining, but I have also watched and listened to those birds sing on cold and rainy days. It used to get on my nerves because they sing so loud. They sing in the sunshine. They sing in the rain. But then I realized one day: their song was never altered by what kind of day it was. ***Tomorrow will be a better day.***

As a person of faith, we believe in the things we cannot see. We believe in God. We believe in eternal life. We believe in the soul of human beings. In the rational world, we believe that one plus one equals two. However, there is something within us that compels us to believe that one plus one also equals three. I believe that unity will one day come from diversity. It is my hope that more of us, will release our blind trust in rules and politics. That we will painfully and faithfully unpack the reality of race, the social construct, that puts one against the other, and begin to see that in the landscape of the US there is really just us. While we all seek to negotiate this short path we call life, may we long to live and love like Jesus, til the war is won.

Pause and Reflect

Take a moment before you move on and think about the following:

Question 1

What has kept you grounded during this season of uncertainty?

____

____

____

____

____

Question 2

Sabbath is more than a day of the week. It is more than a day of worship. It is a command to rest. How are you sanctifying your time?

____

____

____

____

____

Question 3

Courage is the willingness to confront uncertainty. What area of your life is God calling you to face with courage?

____

____

____

____

____

Journal

Think about some of the mountains you have climbed and some of the valleys you have journeyed through. What did these moments teach you about God? What did these moments teach you about yourself?

____

____

____

____

____

____

____

____

____

____

Action

Write a personal affirmation. How do you do this? Write down what you desire. Turn it into a declarative statement. Make sure every word is positive. Write your affirmation using first person. It should only speak to you and about you. Use words like, "I am," "I will," "I can." Avoid negative words. Your affirmation should be ten words or less. Write it and recite it until your spirit receives it. Repeat it daily.

~ Chapter Seven Notes ~

~ CHAPTER EIGHT ~

Affirmations According to Psalm 27

The LORD is my light and my salvation; whom shall I fear? the LORD is the strength of my life; of whom shall I be afraid? When the wicked, even mine enemies and my foes, came upon me to eat up my flesh, they stumbled and fell. Though an host should encamp against me, my heart shall not fear: though war should rise against me, in this will I be confident. One thing have I desired of the LORD, that will I seek after; that I may dwell in the house of the LORD all the days of my life, to behold the beauty of the LORD, and to enquire in his temple. For in the time of trouble he shall hide me in his pavilion: in the secret of his tabernacle shall he hide me; he shall set me up upon a rock. And now shall mine head be lifted up above mine enemies round about me: therefore will I offer in his tabernacle sacrifices of joy; I will sing, yea, I will sing praises unto the LORD. Hear, O LORD, when I cry with my voice: have mercy also upon me, and answer me. When thou saidst, Seek ye my face; my heart said unto thee, Thy face, LORD, will I seek. Hide not thy face far from me; put not thy servant away in anger: thou hast been my help; leave me not, neither forsake me, O God of my salvation. When my father and my mother forsake me, then the LORD will take me up. Teach me thy way, O LORD, and lead me in a plain path, because of mine enemies. Deliver me not over unto the will of mine enemies: for false witnesses are risen up against

> me, and such as breathe out cruelty. I had fainted, unless I had believed to see the goodness of the LORD in the land of the living. Wait on the LORD: be of good courage, and he shall strengthen thine heart: wait, I say, on the LORD. —Psalm 27

Affirmations are popular these days. They are personal development tools that are meant to direct one's thinking toward the positive, rather than focusing on the negative. They are not magic words. Your life is not transformed simply because you say them and repeat them. Affirmations do not change the world around you, but they change the way you see yourself and how you feel about yourself. When you feel different, you think different, and when you think different, you behave different; when you behave different, you get different life results. That is the power of affirmations. The affirmation is designed to change your belief from negative to positive and thereby changing your behavior so that you actually begin to see in your life that which you say with your mouth. As Joel 3:10 declares, "Let the weak say I am strong." The true power of an affirmation is the way it makes you feel and the better beliefs about yourself you are able to form.

Listed below are twenty-one affirmations that I have written according to Psalm 27. I wish to share them with you and to invite you to use these affirmations as morning devotions for the next twenty-one days.

INSTRUCTIONS

1. Repeat each one three times slowly. Do not read them as if you are reading a newspaper or an encyclopedia. Find a quiet, meditative place or posture for reading.
2. Do more than read them. Reflection is important. How might these statements be true in your life? Note your reflections.
3. Read and reflect on one affirmation at a time. This is meant to be a daily exercise in spiritual formation.

TWENTY-ONE DAYS OF MORNING AFFIRMATIONS ACCORDING TO PSALM 27

DAY ONE

I AM GRATEFUL FOR THE PROTECTION OF GOD IN MY LIFE.

Daily Reflections:

____

____

____

____

____

> "The LORD is my light and my salvation; whom shall I fear? the LORD is the strength of my life; of whom shall I be afraid? When the wicked, even mine enemies and my foes, came upon me to eat up my flesh, they stumbled and fell" (vv. 1–2).

DAY TWO

TODAY I WILL WATCH FOR AND WELCOME THE GOOD.

Daily Reflections:

____

____

____

____

____

> "Though an host should encamp against me, my heart shall not fear: though war should rise against me, in this will I be confident" (v. 3).

DAY THREE

MY DESIRES ARE MANIFESTING ON SCHEDULE.

Daily Reflections:

____

____

____

____

____

> "One thing have I desired of the LORD, that will I seek after; that I may dwell in the house of the LORD all the days of my life, to behold the beauty of the LORD, and to enquire in his temple. For in the time of trouble he shall hide me in his pavilion: in the secret of his tabernacle shall he hide me; he shall set me up upon a rock" (vv. 4–5).

DAY FOUR

I WILL ALWAYS LOOK UP BECAUSE GOD IS THE LIFTER OF MY HEAD.

Daily Reflections:

____

____

____

____

____

> "And now shall mine head be lifted up above mine enemies round about me: therefore will I offer in his tabernacle sacrifices of joy; I will sing, yea, I will sing praises unto the LORD" (vv. 6).

DAY FIVE

GOD ALWAYS HEARS MY VOICE.

Daily Reflections:

____

____

____

____

____

> "Hear, O Lord, when I cry with my voice: have mercy also upon me, and answer me. When thou saidst, Seek ye my face; my heart said unto thee, Thy face, Lord, will I seek. Hide not thy face far from me; put not they servant away in anger: thou hast been my help; leave me not, neither forsake me, O God of my salvation. When my father and my mother forsake me, then the Lord will take me up. Teach

me thy way, O Lord, and lead me in a plain path because of mine enemies. Deliver me not over unto the will of mine enemies: for false witnesses are risen up against me, and such as breathe out cruelty" (vv. 7–12).

DAY SIX

I DECREE AND DECLARE HAPPINESS AND SUCCESS.

Daily Reflections:

____

____

____

____

____

> "I had fainted, unless I had believed to see the goodness of the Lord in the land of the living" (v. 13).

DAY SEVEN

I HAVE THE COURAGE TO WAIT ON GOD.

Daily Reflections:

____

____

____

____

____

"Wait on the LORD: be of good courage,
and he shall strengthen thine heart:
wait, I say, on the LORD" (v. 14).

DAY EIGHT

I AM SUFFICIENT IN GOD.

Daily Reflections:

____

____

____

____

____

> "The LORD is my light and my salvation; whom shall I fear? the LORD is the strength of my life; of whom shall I be afraid? When the wicked, even mine enemies and my foes, came upon me to eat up my flesh, they stumbled and fell" (vv. 1–2).

DAY NINE

I FIND COMFORT IN GOD AT ALL TIMES.

Daily Reflections:

____

____

____

____

____

> "Though an host should encamp against me, my heart shall not fear: though war should rise against me, in this will I be confident" (v. 3).

DAY TEN

I AM SAFE, SANE, AND SATISFIED.

Daily Reflections:

____

____

____

____

____

> "One thing have I desired of the LORD, that will I seek after; that I may dwell in the house of the LORD all the days of my life, to behold the beauty of the LORD, and to enquire in his temple. For in the time of trouble he shall hide me in his pavilion: in the secret of his tabernacle shall he hide me; he shall set me up upon a rock" (vv. 4–5).

DAY ELEVEN

I ONLY SEE THE GOOD GOD HAS PREPARED FOR ME.

Daily Reflections:

____

____

____

____

____

> "And now shall mine head be lifted up above mine enemies round about me: therefore will I offer in his tabernacle sacrifices of joy; I will sing, yea, I will sing praises unto the LORD" (v. 6).

DAY TWELVE

I BELONG TO GOD AND NO ONE ELSE.

Daily Reflections:

____

____

____

____

____

> "Hear, O Lord, when I cry with my voice: have mercy also upon me, and answer me. When thou saidst, Seek ye my face; my heart said unto thee, Thy face, Lord, will I seek. Hide not thy face far from me; put not they servant away in anger: thou hast been my help; leave me not, neither forsake me, O God of my salvation. When my father and my mother forsake me, then the Lord will take me up. Teach

me thy way, O Lord, and lead me in a plain path because of mine enemies. Deliver me not over unto the will of mine enemies: for false witnesses are risen up against me, and such as breathe out cruelty" (vv. 7–12).

DAY THIRTEEN

I WILL LIVE TO SEE THE PROMISES OF GOD.

Daily Reflections:

____

____

____

____

____

"I had fainted, unless I had believed to see the goodness of the Lord in the land of the living" (v. 13).

DAY FOURTEEN

I AM GRATEFUL BECAUSE I AM STRONGER.

Daily Reflections:

____

____

____

____

____

"Wait on the LORD: be of good courage, and he shall strengthen thine heart: wait, I say, on the LORD" (v. 14).

DAY FIFTEEN

I AM FOREVER LOVED.

Daily Reflections:

____

____

____

____

____

> "The LORD is my light and my salvation; whom shall I fear? the LORD is the strength of my life; of whom shall I be afraid? When the wicked, even mine enemies and my foes, came upon me to eat up my flesh, they stumbled and fell" (vv. 1–2).

DAY SIXTEEN

I AM FOREVER PROTECTED.

Daily Reflections:

____

____

____

____

____

> "Though an host should encamp against me, my heart shall not fear: though war should rise against me, in this will I be confident" (v. 3).

DAY SEVENTEEN

I AM FOREVER FORGIVEN.

Daily Reflections:

____

____

____

____

____

> "One thing have I desired of the LORD, that will I seek after; that I may dwell in the house of the LORD all the days of my life, to behold the beauty of the LORD, and to enquire in his temple. For in the time of trouble he shall hide me in his pavilion: in the secret of his tabernacle shall he hide me; he shall set me up upon a rock" (vv. 4–5).

DAY EIGHTEEN

I AM RESTORED AND COMPLETE IN GOD.

Daily Reflections:

____

____

____

____

____

> "And now shall mine head be lifted up above mine enemies round about me: therefore will I offer in his tabernacle sacrifices of joy; I will sing, yea, I will sing praises unto the LORD" (v. 6).

DAY NINETEEN

I TRUST THE TIMING OF GOD.

Daily Reflections:

____

____

____

____

____

> "Hear, O Lord, when I cry with my voice: have mercy also upon me, and answer me. When thou saidst, Seek ye my face; my heart said unto thee, Thy face, Lord, will I seek. Hide not thy face far from me; put not they servant away in anger: thou hast been my help; leave me not, neither forsake me, O God of my salvation. When my father and my mother forsake me, then the Lord will take me up. Teach

me thy way, O Lord, and lead me in a plain path because of mine enemies. Deliver me not over unto the will of mine enemies: for false witnesses are risen up against me, and such as breathe out cruelty" (vv. 7–12).

DAY TWENTY

I STAND FIRM IN MY FAITH.

Daily Reflections:

____

____

____

____

____

"I had fainted, unless I had believed to see the goodness of the Lord in the land of the living" (v. 13).

DAY TWENTY-ONE

I WILL REST IN THE PROMISES OF GOD.

Daily Reflections:

____

____

____

____

____

"Wait on the LORD: be of good courage, and he shall strengthen thine heart: wait, I say, on the LORD" (v. 14).

Til The War Is Won

I AM GRATEFUL FOR THE PROTECTION OF GOD IN MY LIFE.

TODAY I WILL WATCH FOR AND WELCOME THE GOOD.

MY DESIRES ARE MANIFESTING ON SCHEDULE.

I WILL ALWAYS LOOK UP BECAUSE GOD IS THE LIFTER OF MY HEAD.

MY VOICE IS ALWAYS HEARD BY GOD.

I DECREE AND DECLARE HAPPINESS AND SUCCESS.

I HAVE THE COURAGE TO WAIT ON GOD.

I AM SUFFICIENT IN GOD.

I FIND COMFORT IN GOD AT ALL TIMES.

I AM SAFE, SANE, AND SATISFIED.

I ONLY SEE THE GOOD GOD HAS PREPARED FOR ME.

I BELONG TO GOD AND NO ONE ELSE.

I WILL LIVE TO SEE THE PROMISES OF GOD.

I AM GRATEFUL BECAUSE I AM STRONGER.

I AM FOREVER LOVED.

I AM FOREVER PROTECTED.

I AM FOREVER FORGIVEN.

I AM RESTORED AND COMPLETE IN GOD.

I TRUST THE TIMING OF GOD.

I STAND FIRM IN MY FAITH.

I WILL REST IN THE PROMISES OF GOD.

About the Author

Dr. McDaniel is an honor graduate of Shaw University where he majored in religion and philosophy and minored in business management. He continued graduate and post-graduate studies at Duke Divinity School, Durham, North Carolina, and at United Theological Seminary in Dayton, Ohio, receiving a Master of Divinity degree and a Doctor of Ministry degree, respectively. In 2007, Pastor McDaniel was invited to Harvard University to participate in a program that focused on economic development and community revitalization. He is an adjunct professor at USC Upstate University where he teaches courses on African American Religious Studies and African American Culture. He is the pastor of Macedonia Missionary Baptist Church in Spartanburg South Carolina. He is the husband of Latron McDaniel and a father of four.

Other books written by Dr. McDaniel are *Live Your Kingdom Life Now: A Theological Guide to Living by Choice Not by Chance* and *If God Be for Us: Pastoral Reflections of Faith and Family Concerning the Black Church.*

CPSIA information can be obtained
at www.ICGtesting.com
Printed in the USA
LVHW111502100921
697523LV00001B/149